PORTSLADE AND HOVE

MEMORIES

JUDY MIDDLETON

SUTTON PUBLISHING

First published in 2004 by
Sutton Publishing Limited · Phoenix Mill
Thrupp · Stroud · Gloucestershire · GL5 2BU

British Library Cataloguing in Publication Data
A catalogue record for this book is available from the British Library

ISBN 0-7509-3991-5

Typeset in 10.5/13pt Galliard.
Typesetting and origination by
Sutton Publishing Limited.
Printed and bound in England by
J.H. Haynes & Co. Ltd, Sparkford.

Contents

Acknowledgements & Author's Note   5

1.   Francis Sclater – Early Days at North House Farm   7

2.   Bert Hyde – Working at North House Farm   11

3.   The Broomfield Family   15

4.   George Steele – An Old-Style Market Garden   19

5.   The Peters Family   25

6.   Peter Simms – Mill House Farm   29

7.   Elsie Peirce – Working at Ronuk   32

8.   Gladys Banfield – From Inskipp's to the
       Wonder of Woolies   38

9.   George Ellis – Butcher's Boy, Baker's
       Roundsman and More   45

10. Miss Austen – A Teacher's Life   49

11. The Tate Family   53

12. Leslie Hamilton – Over Thirty Years a Councillor   58

13. Reg Forrest – A Peashooter at the Picturedrome   62

14. Betty Figg – Life in an Old Cottage   67

15. The Fords – A Family Saga   73

16.   Charlie Todd – Serving in Dad's Army   79

17.   Doug Mepham – A Portslade Gassie   85

18.   Ernest Charles Moore – Life at the Gas Works   91

19.   Frederick Charles Hill of Hill's Radio   96

20.   Eric Masters – Buses, Lorries and a Portslade Childhood   101

21.   Pam Dry – A Friend at Easthill House   107

22.   Desmond Leonard Stevens – From Post Office
          Messenger Boy to REME   110

23.   Thomas Huntley Wood – The Sailor on Player's
          Cigarette Packet   116

24.   Alan Osborne & the Portslade Girl Pipers   119

25.   Norman Daniel Shaw of Shaw's Stores   124

26.   The Woolgar Family   133

27.   John Bryon – Childhood Days at Hove   140

28.   Arthur Henry Collins – Working on the *Hove Echo*   145

29.   Joyce Hopkins – Old Hove Street   149

30.   Vera Messenger – Parlour Maid to
          General Gordon's Niece   155

31.   Frank Mainstone – the Duke of Portland's Bailiff   157

       Index   158

Author's Note & Acknowledgements

This book is compiled from *Memories of Old Portslade* (1990) and *More Memories of Old Portslade* (1991), which appeared as self-published booklets in a run of no more than 100 copies each. In addition there are new memories, including some from Hove.

It would not have been possible without the help and lively reminiscences of many people – my thanks to them all.

They are Gladys Banfield, John Broomfield, John Bryon, Brenda Buck, Mrs E. Chambers, Miss J. Collins, Pam Dry, George Ellis, Betty Figg, Don Gates, Dorothy Gedye, Archie Greenyer, Joyce Hopkins, Les Hamilton, Olive Hamilton, Mrs J. Hayward, Andrew Hill, Frederick Charles Hill, Bert and Gladys Hyde, Robert Jeeves, Eric Masters, Vera Messenger, Alan Osborne, Elsie Peirce, Cecil and Doris Peters, Daphne Perrin, Norman Shaw, Mr and Mrs G. Steele, Peter Simms, Desmond Leonard Stevens, John Tate, Charlie Todd, Mr R.A. Uridge, Mrs K. Ward and Bill Woolgar.

1

Francis Sclater

Early Days at North House Farm

Francis Sclater went to work at North House Farm in 1922 – just after he left school – and he stayed until 1925. I never interviewed him and the following details were gleaned from some typewritten sheets that Francis put together at the request of his friend Dick Uridge, who in turn allowed me to look at them in January 1991.

When Francis went to work at the farm it was run under the partnership of John Broomfield and Sidney West. Each man had his particular interest – Broomfield was responsible for the milking herd up at Easthill together with the cattle, sheep and arable land, while West's baby was the market garden land in the valley at Mile Oak. West was a firm believer in the benefits of a cold bath every morning, and as Francis lived in the farmhouse during the week, he was obliged to follow suit. It was not an experience he enjoyed on a frosty morning.

Horses were a part of the working world of farm life. There were four or five teams working the land and some fine horses for pulling the delivery van to Brighton market. West's cob called Topsy was used for the delicate task of hoeing in the market garden, while at other times she was harnessed to his dog-cart. Bob, Jane, Laddie and Herbert (the latter pronounced without the 'H') were the names of some of the other horses about the farm. They were well fed and well looked after. Francis used to ride one of them home to Newick every weekend to see his family. Sid had another horse called Commie and then there was the big shire called Jolly. Poor Jolly came to an unfortunate end. Outside the stables there was a lovely patch of green grass, but nobody realised that underneath was a deep well covered only by sleepers. Jolly was decked out in his full harness and was being led round for a foot inspection, when there was a sudden rumble and he disappeared backwards into a large hole – all of 50 or 60ft deep. On the farm plan this well was shown as having been filled in. The accident had to be reported to the Water Authority, as Mile Oak was a source of pure water and the company insisted on the corpse being removed. It was a monumental undertaking, even with a strong winch and chains, and the farmhands had to jump on the base of the winch to stop it rising as poor Jolly's weight threatened to wrench it up.

Some of Broomfield's sheep enclosed within hurdles made from woven hazel, 1935. (Broomfield)

However, horsepower was not the only source of energy on the farm. There were two large steam engines that remained stationary at either side of a field, pulling the plough or cultivator from one side to the other. Three old chaps ran the contraption and they were based in a little hut on wheels (similar to the old-time shepherd's hut) that travelled with them from field to field.

The farmhands were a friendly bunch and Francis described them as real country lads. They were Big Joe, Jack Banfield (nicknamed Banny), Jack Tester, Old Arthur (who had a high pitched voice and rode an old grey mare) and young Puggle. It was Puggle who was leading Jolly when he fell down the well, and it was fortunate that he was not dragged down with the horse. These men drove the van loaded with market produce to Brighton every day, leaving the farm at 5 a.m. They returned carrying a full load of horse dung collected from various stables en route.

Mill Mower lived at the farmhouse too. He was the farm carpenter – a little eccentric but skilled at his trade. Little Joey also lived there. He was the son of Big Joe and looked after West's cob Topsy. The carter, whose team worked on the farm, was Mr Standing. At New Barn Farm the carter was Wag Hilton, and his horses always looked particularly healthy with gleaming coats. Wag let Francis into his secret remedy for keeping the shine on their coats – it was to mix urine in with their feed, and Wag concluded darkly, 'maid's water is best!'

There was a large flock of sheep – big Oxford Down Cross specimens – and a full-time shepherd to look after them with the assistance of under-shepherd Fred. Charley had a quaint phrase for when the rams were sent in with the ewes – he called it 'knitting time'.

The sheep were dipped in the yard at Mile Oak. The dipping bath was made of wood with a sort of table at one end. The sheep were lifted on to the table on their backs and then immersed into the bath. Great care was taken to keep their heads above water. West favoured a rather powerful dip powder and insisted all hands (who were pretty well drenched anyway) should wash themselves afterwards in a circular tub of cold water. When it was sheep-washing time, the flock was taken over the Downs to Fulking where a spring gushed out at the roadside. It was an established practice that the shepherds made a dam on the road before proceeding to wash the sheep. The spring water was freezing cold and it was limb-numbing work, so naturally, afterwards a pint or two at the Shepherd and Dog was very welcome. It was no easy matter to ensure everyone got home safely, including the sheep. West and Francis would ride over to lend a hand.

The Southdown Foxhounds used to meet at the farm towards the end of the season. In 1924 Moffat Smith was still Master, Joe Mackarness was Huntsman, and

North House Farm when the Southdown Foxhounds met there, 1924. Joe Mackarness (Mack), the Huntsman, is seen mounted on the left. (Uridge)

George Lloyd and Bill Windley were whippers-in. A glass of cherry brandy was provided to the participants to warm them up beforehand. Francis filled the role of official earth-stopper. This entailed scouting the land looking for earths and blocking them up. For every find he earned 10s, but it was not an easy task because there were large patches of prickly gorse on Cockroost Hill, the Dyke Hovel and Fulking Furze. West and Francis often attended meets of the Southdown Foxhounds that took place at Henfield, Poynings and Albourne. It was a pleasant ride over the Downs to these places. There was hardly anything to obstruct their passage, and if there was any wire, it was marked with a red flag.

When Francis returned home to Newick at the weekends, the ride took him about 3½ hours. He rode to Devil's Dyke, down to Saddlescombe, up and over to Pycombe, along past Jack and Jill windmills to Ditchling Beacon and on to Plumpton Borstal, then down to the Half Moon and so on. His father used to tell Francis's faithful old terrier Fixie that he was on his way and Fixie waited on the lawn. As soon as he saw the horse, Fixie rushed to meet them, leaping up to ride on the front of the saddle. On Monday mornings Francis left home at 3 a.m. so as to be in time to meet West and Broomfield in the yard and find out the day's work. Once West reported that there were cockroaches in his scullery, so he asked Francis to bring him back a couple of hedgehogs. This he managed to do – all the way from Newick in a sack – and they did the trick.

West and Francis struck up a firm friendship, and when West retired and went to live in Burgess Hill, Francis often used to visit him from Newick.

2

Bert Hyde

Working at North House Farm

Bert Hyde was born in 1909 at Rudgwick, where his father worked as a stockman. The family later moved to Ashurst, near Steyning. It so happened that working on this farm with Hyde Snr was a Mr Goacher, whose daughter Gladys had been born in Portslade. In 1933 Mr Goacher decided he would like to return to Portslade and work at North House Farm, owned by John Broomfield, and that was how Bert and Gladys Hyde came to live here too. They married in 1935.

North House Farm covered much of the land now occupied by Valley Road and the neighbouring streets. During the years Bert developed a number of different skills. He started work at 6 a.m., milking three cows by hand, perched on a traditional three-legged stool. The milk-pails were carried to the farmhouse where some of the milk was made into butter.

Bert also tended the market gardens where a variety of vegetables, such as potatoes, carrots, sprouts and turnips, were grown. There were greenhouses for the tomatoes and a good spread of gooseberry and blackcurrant bushes. There was no need to spread nets over the fruit bushes, because they grew near the farmhouse, so there was enough activity going on to keep marauding birds at bay. Neither were the vegetables sprayed with insecticide. The only application was manure, of which there was a copious supply, as there were two cattle yards at Easthill and another at New England, besides the cattle at North House Farm. Another source was the output from Trigwell's piggeries at Mile Oak, and Mr Trigwell was not averse to slinging the odd dead pig into the compost heap. It was all forked in.

In the fields, wheat, barley and oats were grown. Much of this went into feeding the cattle. Bert had the task of grinding up the stuff and dishing it out. He also took care of the horses, which were still used to pull the plough in a team of two. In the old days oxen were in use at Portslade. But ploughing with animals soon became nothing but a memory, and by the 1950s Bert had learned to drive a Massey Ferguson tractor.

Another of Bert's skills was the making and thatching of haystacks. First of all he would build up the stack, which was then left to settle for two weeks. Then, thatching began. He used straw to do the job rather than the reeds used to thatch a domestic dwelling. The thatch was secured to the stack with a number of

Bert Hyde with Monty, 1945. (Hyde)

spars, which he fashioned himself. A horizontal bar was fixed around the haystack wall and the spars were twisted and inserted vertically on the bar at regular intervals. This kept the whole structure tight.

During the Second World War there was more than enough labour on the farm, because as well as the land girls there were also some German PoWs who came over daily from Shoreham. It fell to Bert to instruct them on what needed to be done. For instance, in one field he had to explain that the red plants were the tops of beetroot and must be left alone while the green bits and pieces were weeds and must be pulled up.

One land girl had an ardent suitor who landed his biplane in a nearby field and wanted to whisk his beloved away there and then. But Bert refused to allow it and that was that. On another occasion he noticed a British plane flying low over Portslade; it was obviously damaged because it could not lower its wheels. So the pilot cushioned his landing by coming down on top of one of Bert's precious haystacks, climbing out unharmed. But it was not all good news for Bert, because while the pilot went off to have a well-earned sleep at the farm, he was obliged to stand guard over the aircraft all night long. Otherwise, eager souvenir hunters would have stripped the plane before the authorities could examine it.

Bert worked at North House Farm for forty years with three generations of the Broomfields as bosses. Old John Broomfield started off his farming career with 4 rented acres, and in 1901 he moved to North House Farm. Bert recalls a rather sad conversation he had with old John Broomfield as they walked through the fields one day. 'Do you know, Bert,' he said, 'they want all this bally ground from me.' He never swore and 'bally' was the closest he came to bad language when he was annoyed. Land was needed for a new school and council housing. Portslade Council made an offer for some of Broomfield's land. But he was outraged at the prospect of his lovely farmland being swamped by housing, and he refused. He meant to fight. But in the end there was not much he could do, since the council slapped a compulsory purchase order on the land it wanted and then added insult to injury by paying him a lower figure than had been offered in the first place.

Nevertheless, life at the farm was busy and varied. Bert enjoyed the company and used to have breakfast at the farmhouse every morning. He came to know all the Broomfields well and he can remember the time when Amy, Albert's twin sister, became very annoyed with her brother. The cause of the argument is lost in the mists of time, but Albert ended by telling her she was lucky to live on the fat of the land. Amy took her revenge at breakfast time the next morning. Bert knew what was in store and tried to stop Amy, but when he saw his efforts were useless, he beat a diplomatic retreat. Anyway, Amy was waiting behind the kitchen door, and as her brother came in, she emptied a whole bowl of cream over his head with the retort 'There, now you can have some of the fat of the land yourself!'

Although Bert enjoyed his working life, his wife Gladys felt her life was a hard grind with continuous scrimping, and she certainly does not look back on those times through rose-tinted spectacles. Her husband's wages were 32*s* a week, and out of that the rent had to be paid. There were perks such as free milk and free coal – the latter being delivered at the rate of 1cwt one week and 2cwt the next, which worked out at about 3cwt a fortnight. It was hard to make ends meet, and she often urged him to seek higher wages elsewhere. However, he was quite happy where he was. So Gladys went out to work, juggling that with running the home and bringing up their daughter Audrey. Gladys used to scrub the floor of the George in the morning. Then she went to help Mrs Huggett in her large house opposite North Road, before going to help in the tobacconist and sweet shop in South Street. She remembered going without quite often so that Audrey could be properly fed and clothed.

The Hydes' first married home in Portslade was a large flat in Brasslands Drive. Gladys loved it there with its wide views sweeping down to the sea. After five years they moved to 31 High Street – a transfer neither wished to make. The reason was Bill Cook, another Broomfield worker, who took it into his head that he wanted the Hydes living next door to him. So he went to see Mr Broomfield about it and as Mr Broomfield said to Bert, 'I always do what he wants.' He had a soft spot for Bill because they had grown up together.

The house at 31 High Street was primitive to say the least. There was no bathroom or inside loo, lighting was by gas and the cooking was done on an old coal-fired range – the yard at the back was tiny too. On top of it all, the place was damp and the only consolation was that the rent was 4*s* a week, which meant a saving of 10*s* a week compared to what they had paid for the Brasslands Drive flat. There was an additional hazard during the Second

Bert Hyde drives a Massey Ferguson tractor, 1945. (Hyde)

Audrey Hyde in her capacious pram outside Easthill Cottage, 1941. (Hyde)

World War when there were French Canadians stationed nearby. Gladys used to feel very vulnerable as they rolled out of the Stag or the George after a convivial evening. Sometimes they tried to get into the house and even made an attempt to scale the high fence at the back.

At length the Hydes grew fond of the house and various improvements were carried out. They lived there for thirty-five years. But the first fifteen years were spent without the benefit of electricity. In the 1950s they grew rather fed up with this state of affairs, especially when so many friends were enjoying having television. Bert went so far as to hand in his notice, saying that he was going to work at Easthill instead. Of course Mr Broomfield wanted to know the real reason, and when he learned it was because of the lack of electricity he said, 'Don't worry, it will be laid on shortly.' And it was.

The Broomfield Family

The Broomfields have been farmers for generations and can trace their family tree in Sussex back to the seventeenth century. A branch of the family came to Portslade in about 1840. John Broomfield was born in 1868 in Portslade Grange, but as a child he lived in Smokey House. He started his farming career on a small holding called Four Acres – the site is now covered by the back gardens of the houses in Southdown Road. He moved to North House Farm in 1901, and eventually he was farming Stonery Farm and Mile Oak Farm, both of which he owned, and Easthill Farm, which he rented from Brighton Corporation. Not counting Mile Oak Farm, he farmed about 300 acres. There is some confusion about Mile Oak Farm – Edward Blaker sold 294 acres to Brighton Corporation in 1890 and John Broomfield sold some more to Brighton Corporation Waterworks in the 1920s.

John Broomfield with cups he won at three separate agricultural shows for Best Butcher's Beast, 1936. (Broomfield)

Land girls at Portslade, 1917. Amy Broomfield is perched on the right, while cousin Harry balances on top. (Greenfield)

John Broomfield always maintained that parts of the Downs were farmed long before they were ploughed up during the Second World War. He had farmed the land, including Cockroost Hill, almost as far north as the Dyke. It was the depression of the 1930s that led to intensive farming being abandoned for a while. Farming was often a somewhat hazardous enterprise and there was the famous example when John decided to sow 40 acres of cauliflower in Benfield Valley. It proved an excellent crop, but unfortunately there was a glut on the market at the time and he was unable to sell them. There were happier occasions, such as in 1936 when he won silver cups for Best Butcher's Beast at three different agricultural shows.

John Broomfield married Amy Dearing and they had four children – Albert, Amy, Maurice and Frank. Frank was the third child, he died in 1920 from war injuries. The twins Albert and Amy were born in 1898 – she was famous for her volatile temper. Family and farm-workers learned to read the weather signs by looking at her face. If she was in a bad mood, they might not get any breakfast. John Broomfield's grandson, also called John, told a variation of the cream story mentioned in the previous chapter. Apparently, young Broomfield had been despatched to Haywards Heath market to buy some house cows – that is young cows for the exclusive use of the household. But he did not like the look of any of the young calves and returned home empty-handed. Amy was furious. She was standing in the kitchen attending to a large pot, which contained 4 gallons of clotted cream, and at the same time having a good old moan to Albert. As she grumbled she flicked some dollops of cream at her brother's face. He, in his turn, was so angry that he lifted up the pot and emptied the contents over Amy's head. Amy never married, but she enjoyed life and was quite an independent spirit. She worked as a land girl in the First World War, in the thirties she went skiing in Switzerland, and she took a trip to Buenos Aires aboard a large luxury liner.

John was something of a patriarch, and he would not allow his sons to strike out on their own, insisting they help out on the farms. Albert was desperate to go to sea, and he must have passed something of his thwarted longing on to his own sons. But he remained dutifully at home. He was a member of Portslade Council for twenty-one years. In April 1937 he came top of the polls with 596 votes, but it was also a fraught year for him because he had to leave the meetings every time the topic of buying 25 acres north of Chalky Road from him and joint owner Sid West came up for discussion. In 1953 he was elected chairman of Portslade Council.

Maurice made a bolt for freedom by enlisting in 1916. But he lied about his age. When his mother wrote to his commanding officer revealing his true age, he was sent back home to Portslade where he continued working for his father at North House Farm. He married Mabel Gertrude Turner, who was born at the Mile Oak Waterworks where her father Samuel Turner was the resident engineer. She and his sister Amy had been friends and contemporaries at

Peter Broomfield wearing the uniform of Hove High School, which was at Clarendon Villas. (Broomfield)

Johnny Cole and John Broomfield in the snow, c. 1936. The farmhouse is in the background. (Broomfield)

Bill Patching ploughing at North House Farm in the 1940s. (Brighton & Hove Libraries)

St Nicolas's School, which for young Mabel meant a 2-mile walk every school day. Maurice died in 1972.

Albert Broomfield was a Tory councillor until the Portslade Race Track affair blew up. In the 1930s there were moves to create a motor-racing track on the Downs at Portslade. Albert was all in favour of the idea, thinking it would bring prestige and all kinds of business into the area. But the residents of Benfield were horrified at the idea and told Albert that if he continued to support the scheme, they would not vote for him. He refused to be browbeaten and stood as an independent councillor henceforth.

He married a Miss Godwin and they had two sons, Peter (who was born in 1922) and John (who was born in 1925). They inherited their father's love of the sea. Peter joined the Royal Navy and John served for four years in the Merchant Navy during the Second World War, after which John was quite happy to settle back on the family farm, but he kept sailing as a leisure interest. In 1979 he took part in the gruelling 2,400-mile race to the Azores and back in his yacht *Morning Shot*, which he built. He was a member of the Sussex Yacht Club and the Portslade and West Hove Rotary Club. Young John Broomfield lived at the Stonery for forty years and he was convinced that the place was haunted. When he retired he moved to a house in Hove, south of New Church Road. His children were Philip and Julia, and in the 1990s his son-in-law was still farming in Portslade. John Broomfield died on 15 July 1999 and his funeral was held at St Nicolas's Church, on 23 July.

Some of the Broomfields' land was the subject of a compulsory purchase order in the 1930s. Although Albert and Maurice Broomfield were Portslade councillors, they could not vote on the issue because they had a vested interest and the motion to acquire the land by compulsory purchase was passed by seven votes to six.

George Steele

An Old-Style Market Garden

George Steele is descended from market gardeners on both sides of the family. However, his great-grandfather spent all his working life at the windmill on Easthill and he lived in Mill Cottages, at the top of Foredown. George's grandfather, also Alfred Steele, was ninety-five years old when he died in 1942, and so it must have been in about 1847 when he was born in Mill Cottages. Alfred and his son Henry were both market gardeners, but strangely enough Henry did not want his sons to follow in his footsteps. George was born in 1906 in a house on the west side of Crown Villa in Old Shoreham Road (since demolished for road widening). There were two brothers in the family and a sister who was seven years younger than the second boy. Later, the family moved to Rose Cottage, a house in a row of three on the corner of Abinger Road and Gardener Street. There was a fine garden at the front – filled not with roses but with dahlias – and a small yard at the back.

The fact that Henry Steele worked on the land was a bonus for his family during the First World War. When food became scarce, the Steeles were never without a good supply of vegetables for the table, including potatoes, which at times were unavailable in the shops. Their bread was delivered daily from Still's Bakery in lower Portslade. George's favourite snack was a slice of bread with condensed milk poured over it. There was also plenty of bread and dripping to fill in the gaps later in the day.

Besides his trade as a gardener, Henry was an expert at killing chickens quickly. He thought that animals should not suffer unnecessarily, and with a deft flick of his wrist he would break a chicken's neck cleanly. He was much in demand before Christmas by people who had reared their own birds for the table but did not have the stomach for the kill. Henry had the same dexterity in despatching rabbits. Going rabbiting on the Downs for the pot was a popular sport. There was a well-established rabbit warren on the other side of Truleigh Hill, going down to Beeding. Part of it was fenced off and protected, but anybody could take a rabbit from the old warren on the left. There were also numerous rabbits to be found in the countryside running north from Mile Oak Waterworks.

When the rabbits were dead, the next task was to paunch them, that is, to slit the front and remove the entrails, which were buried. From the age of ten George could do this and skin a rabbit as well as anybody else. He was not the slightest bit squeamish about this aspect of country life, and would quite happily hand over a rabbit or chicken to his father to be killed.

Pig killing was another matter, since it required four men to do the job. We need not touch on the gory details, but suffice it to say that the pig sensed what was in store and set up an almighty squealing. Then all the other pigs in the neighbourhood would join in too.

But to return to the less traumatic acres of a market garden. Henry worked for Abraham Peters, an amiable fellow who enjoyed a few drinks. When Abraham retired, Henry Steele went to work for his brother, John Peters. The Peters's had land in Portslade as well as renting a large stretch along where Manor Hall Road is today. Both Henry and his father worked for John Peters, and young George would lend a hand too so that there were three generations working on the land at the same time. Henry was also allowed his own plot of land on which to grow vegetables for his family.

The Peterses kept their three large work-horses in stables at Abinger Road. They were used for ploughing or for taking the produce to Brighton market. George enjoyed accompanying his father to market now and then; and the horses enjoyed it too – becoming quite excited at leaving the stables in the middle of the night. The cart had to leave Portslade at 2 a.m. with a paraffin lamp hung at either side. George perched up among the produce and usually dozed off because it was a slow progress to Brighton with Henry walking at the horse's head. But by 6 a.m. the vegetables would be heaped up on the pavement at Bartholomews, the horse would be in a stable until needed later, and the greengrocers would begin their tour of inspection. Some greengrocers carted away the produce themselves, but others wanted it delivered to their shops. Before the journey back, there was a welcome adjournment to Lowe's shop, a tea-shop in Bartholomews where large mugs of tea and thick sandwiches could be purchased. They would not return until lunchtime, and the same procedure was followed three times a week – on Tuesdays, Thursdays and Saturdays. A carter earned more money than a man who just worked in the market garden all day.

Henry was also the seedsman, and he was very possessive about his box drill. It was stored in a shed when not in use, but nobody else was allowed to touch it. Inside the wooden box, there was a spindle and a brush, and Henry used to paint the funnel chalk-white so that it was easy to see if the seed was falling correctly. You could adjust the rate of flow.

It is interesting to note that sea kale was grown – a crop you rarely hear about today. It was a luxury item as it required careful tending. It was grown under a covering of manure 3 to 4ins thick. At a certain stage the manure had to be removed and straw put down instead – it was the straight, fleshy, white shoots that were prized. Sea kale was not allowed to sprout into curly leaves at the top – these leaves could be eaten, but they were apt to be tough. Sea kale was quite bland, but Henry's wife had a special recipe for cooking it in a type of bread sauce.

One charming aspect of the old-style market garden was the row of alcoves, each about 12ft square, with one containing a marrow plant and the next a cucumber.

Harvesters at work in south Portslade. Many families found the seasonal work a useful source of income. (Osborne)

The marrows and cucumbers did not require sunlight so much as warmth and on the inside of each bower early peas were planted with runner beans on the outside. As the latter grew, they provided warmth and protection. An added help to the marrow and cucumber seedlings was the application of oiled paper. During the winter Henry used to take stacks of old newspapers to his garden shed and painstakingly paint each sheet with linseed oil. First of all the seeds were planted, then two withies were arched across them and upon them two sheets of oiled paper. When the seedlings reached paper height, holes were made for them, but the paper was left where it was.

Caterpillars were the biggest problem. Action had to be taken or else the crop would be ruined. But it was a tedious task stumping along the rows, plucking off caterpillars and dropping them in a bucket. It helped if the vegetables were doused in salty water. In hot, dry summers flea-beetles were a nuisance too. As you walked by the vegetables you could hear them clicking. They liked to bore little holes in the small green crops as well as in turnips and radishes. Rooks were another major problem. They had a trick of pulling up pea seedlings and eating the pea at the end. Given the chance they could strip whole rows in no time at all. There was nothing for it but to employ a young boy as a rook scarer, either by banging on a tin, or by using a proper wooden rattle.

George went to St Nicolas's School. He was one of the lucky ones, as some children were so poor they did not have shoes and so were unable to attend. After school during the First World War George and his friends used to hang around the gap in the hedge at Locks Hill, because in the field below there were soldiers billeted in white bell tents. Quite often the soldiers would be feeling in a generous mood, and once George came home with a large tin of Australian apricot jam with the legend 'IXL' on the label. He could recall the marvellous taste of that jam many years later. Another time he was given a loaf of bread, which he quickly pushed inside his blue school jumper and ran all the way home with it – perhaps he was afraid some other child might steal it from him.

Soon many Portslade families were on more familiar terms with the soldiers. There was a bad storm and the camp was flooded out. The officers then marched around the neighbourhood, knocking on every door and enquiring how many rooms there were and how many people occupied the house. The residents had no choice in the matter. The Steeles found themselves playing host to three soldiers who shared a bed in the middle bedroom. The baby girl moved in with her parents and the two boys squashed up together in the small bedroom known as the slip room.

However, there were consolations, such as extra rations and 1s a day paid for each soldier. They were really no bother, getting up early in the morning and spending most of the day away. They only stayed until huts had been erected for them on the camp site and then they were gone.

But Florence Reed, who was later to marry George Steele, and whose family were also market gardeners, had soldiers billeted with her for the whole of the war. The Reeds lived at Southwick, although they were a Portslade family. Florence's grandfather, William Reed, used to live in a large house called the Stonery and worked on the market garden there.

George recalled that when the soldiers were billeted in the houses, pay-day was quite a spectacle. The paymaster marched to their road, accompanied by soldiers bearing a folding table and chair. These were plonked on the pavement, the dignified paymaster took his seat and the soldiers lined up for their pay.

The Royal Engineers encamped on part of the playing fields belonging to Windlesham House School, which was requisitioned by the Army in 1914. (Hayward)

Above: *Market gardener Harry Reed with his bride Ivy Jones, May 1941. His sister Florence is the bridesmaid. Wartime restrictions meant that there was not the cloth available to make or buy new wedding outfits, so Ivy and Florence had to borrow their dresses. (Steele)*

Below: *William Reed married Joan Biulderbeck at St Nicolas's Church, Portslade, on 7 June 1947. Florence Reed is bridesmaid again. The somewhat gaunt bridegroom had recently been demobbed after wartime service in the Royal Signals. (Steele)*

George Herbert Steele married Florence Reed at St Nicolas's Church on 16 October 1948. The whole family chipped in with clothing coupons for her outfit. The couple met while serving in the wartime Civil Defence. (Steele)

George thought he would like to leave school at the earliest opportunity in 1918 – not that he was unhappy there – he just wanted to earn some money. So quite independently, he applied to take the labour examination, which schoolchildren were allowed to take at twelve years of age, provided they had reached standard six. George had to go to St Andrew's School, Portslade, where a government inspector was waiting to examine him in reading, writing, arithmetic, history and geography. George passed. But when his father got to hear about it, he put his foot down and insisted George stay on at school. He only relented at Easter when George was thirteen and a half and had the offer of a job in Hector Read's shop at Southern Cross. It was situated at the top of Bampfield Street. George's wages were 8*s* a week and the hours were from 8 a.m. to 7 p.m. on Mondays, Tuesdays and Thursdays; 8 a.m. to 8 p.m. on Fridays; 8 a.m. to 9 p.m. on Saturdays and there was a half-day on Wednesday. Goodness knows why Henry Steele thought it would be an easier life than working in a market garden.

5

The Peters Family

The Peterses were a very numerous family at Portslade, and it seems that they were there from the 1750s. In the 1852 *Sussex Directory* under Portslade twenty-two traders were listed, of which seven were Peterses. They were William and Francis Peters, millers; Charles Peters, carrier and post office receiving house; Mrs Charlotte Peters, butcher; Edwin Peters, baker; Thomas Peters collector of taxes and George Peters, cow-keeper and occupier of the George Inn. The family was also connected with other pubs in Portslade. In 1841 William Peters ran the Bull Inn, and he was still there in 1861 (the pub was probably renamed the Stag's Head); Martin James Peters was the landlord of the Jolly Sailors in Wellington Road from at least 1873; Thomas Peters ran the Southern Cross in the 1880s; James Peters kept the Railway Inn in 1891 and in 1892 Thomas Peters was landlord of the Gardener's Arms.

But the Peterses also branched out into market gardening with Abraham Peters cultivating some 11 acres in south Portslade from 1859. Harry Peters, who lived in Alma Cottage, was also a market gardener, as was his son Frederick. Later this same Frederick became foreman of the paint shop at Portslade Gas Works. However, when he was laid off because of injury, he became depressed and committed suicide. He waited until his wife was having a night out at the pictures and then he gassed himself. Unfortunately, his eleven-year-old son Cecil discovered his body. When the inquest was held at Portslade fire station, the coroner ordered that 5*s* should be given to Cecil for coping so well and doing all the right things at the scene of the tragedy.

Cecil was born in 1915 at 29 Elm Road, Portslade. His arrival was probably something of a shock because his mother was forty-five and his father fifty-five. There were already three sons and a daughter, as well as a step-sister from his father's first marriage. Cecil's brother Fred served in the East Surrey Regiment during the First World War and was killed on 1 November 1918, ten days before the Armistice. Cecil's sister Cecilia, known as Cissie, married Len Grigson, one of a brood of thirteen children from 49 Abinger Road. Their only child Kathleen was born brain-damaged. They kept her at home until she died aged twenty-one, and a year later Cissie, no doubt worn out by the constant caring, died of a tumour.

Cecil's mother used to work in the evenings at Dudeney's Laundry on the corner of Shelldale Road and Abinger Road. She excelled at the ironing board and in the use of the goffering tongs, and so she was given the task of ironing all the little frilly

The Peters family at the back of 29 Elm Road, Portslade, 1918. Young Cecil sits on his mother's knee. (Peters)

A wedding group outside Cowhayes Farm, Portslade, 1919, when Albert Goacher married Miss Harwood – her father stands on the left. Cecil Peters is the somewhat glum little boy dressed in the sailor suit at the front. (Peters)

Fred Peters of the East Surrey Regiment was killed on 1 November 1918, just ten days before the Armistice. (Peters)

Cissie Peters and Dorothy Oden, c. 1908. Dorothy's parents ran a bakery shop at 95 Abinger Road. (Peters)

Cissie Peters and Len Grigson on their wedding day, c. *1921. (Peters)*

aprons and caps worn by female staff at the top Brighton hotels. She used the old-fashioned flat iron for more mundane articles.

Cecil was educated at St Nicolas's School and left at fourteen to become an apprentice mechanic. In 1940 he was called up into the Royal Engineers, graduating to the 10th Bomb Disposal Company. He was posted to Sheffield, and it was there that he met his future wife Doris. They became engaged when she was nineteen and they were married in Sheffield. Although the happy pair returned to Elm Road, Portslade, Doris went back to Sheffield for the birth of Carol on Boxing Day 1945. But Cecil and Doris were later delighted when they were allocated a prefab in Denmark Road, Portslade.

Cecil's Uncle Tom was brought up in Alma Cottage, where he was born in 1866. By 1906 Tom had two pretty teenage daughters called Florence and May. One Saturday evening they went on a boat trip on the canal with their boyfriends. But a sudden squall blew up, overturning the boat and drowning the sisters. Their boyfriends survived. On the day of the funeral the local newspaper recorded that 'little knots of sympathisers reverently raised their hats as the cortège passed through the streets, and St Andrew's Church was crowded to overflowing. Women sobbed quietly through the service, and in drenching rain a great number of people marched behind the mourners' coaches to the Portslade Cemetery. Conspicuous in the procession was a cart laden with beautiful wreaths.' One sister remained, and she married a Mr Davis who taught at Portslade Industrial School. He was a big, red-faced man who was fond of propping up the bar at the Stag's Head.

Peter Simms

Mill House Farm

Mill House Farm was situated between where Mill Lane and Helena Close are today. Edward Blaker owned the land in the nineteenth century, and the trustees of his will sold it at auction on 21 October 1895 for £520.

By 1930 G.W. Jones owned Mill House Farm and the lessee was Mrs E. Bramwell Davies. The promoter W.R. Kells came up with the marvellous idea of staging whippet racing at the farm. While this might have been popular with ordinary folk, the neighbours were appalled. In September 1930 Mrs E. Webb of Easthill House complained about the whippet racing and the following month the Revd Noel E.C. Hemsworth, vicar of St Nicolas's Church, followed suit. He objected especially to whippet racing being held on Sundays, and this also brought down the wrath of the Lord's Day Observance Society upon Mr Kells. The society promised urgent action, and although Portslade Council was in favour of the move, they did not provide any cash to back the scheme. The council considered that whippet racing disturbed the peace and the barking and yapping interfered with religious services, while there would be an influx of noisy and undesirable people who were inclined to use profane language. In October 1931 the Lord's Day Observance Society informed Portslade Council that whippet racing at Mill House Farm had now ceased and the lease surrendered to the freeholders, whose solicitors stated they had no intention of holding more meetings.

According to Peter Simms (now resident in Canada) his father, R.F. Simms, purchased Mill House Farm from an American during the 1940s when the property was still occupied by Canadian soldiers. The accommodation consisted of two eighteenth-century flint-built cottages, plus a modern wing, all linked together to form one dwelling. The contrast between the old cottages and the modern wing was considerable – the ceilings in the cottages were low and the rooms small, whereas the new wing had high ceilings and there was a 35ft long living room. The owners lived in the recent part while servants lived in the old cottages. The Simms family moved there in 1947. South of the cottages were stables for three horses and two rooms known as the ostler's quarters. South of the stables was a huge flint building with forty iron rings embedded in the walls for securing the horses. The property covered 3 acres with a frontage to the west. On the west side there was an old flint wall and a row of giant fir trees while a 12ft brick wall bounded the north, south and east sides. On entering at the front gates there was a full-sized tennis court to the left and a sunken garden to the right. There was a lavender garden, a large vegetable garden and an orchard to the east of the buildings. The orchard contained over 200 apple trees. The apples were stored in four special rooms fitted with sliding shelves about 6ins apart, which had been constructed at the entrance to the cottage side. The greenhouse contained two vines, one producing black grapes and the other white, while beside the windmill a greengage tree and a cherry flourished. There was a potting shed nearby and in front of the greenhouse a functioning well fitted with a cover. Ducks, chickens and geese roamed freely throughout the grounds.

The remains of the windmill were situated north of the modern wing and consisted of one large, circular room, which was completely dry and serviceable. Mr Simms made it into a house in 1948 with a spiral staircase leading to a newly constructed second floor. When the Canadians occupied the site during the war they kept their Army trucks in the large granary, while a tank or Bren gun carrier was parked in the entrance. As the latter was too wide to go through the gates, part of the old flint wall had to come down or was removed by the vehicle. Stacks of ammunition were stored in the Mill House and the modern living room was turned into a skating rink – the windows were removed and then the wooden floor was

Peter's brother Richard is in the pram with his cousin Michael standing on the right in the gardens of Mill House. The other children are Rodney and Delia Smart. (Simms)

Richard Simms and Jennifer Delfoss playing with a rather splendid model horse and carriage in the grounds of Mill House. The Delfoss family used to live in Southwick, but emigrated to Canada in 1953. (Simms)

flooded. The Canadians managed to get some skates from somewhere and it was even rumoured that they managed to play ice hockey when it was cold enough.

When the Canadians moved on they left behind some brand new billycans, which young Peter Simms distributed to the other boys in his Scout patrol. Chewing gum wrappers were found everywhere – mostly a brand called Sweet Sixteen, which was a cinnamon-flavoured gum. After the war two mines were discovered in the sunken garden and sappers were called in to clear them. The event caused quite a bit of excitement.

Mr Simms experienced some trouble with his tenants. Eventually he had to pay them a great deal of money to vacate the premises. Then the family business was nationalised and he decided to emigrate to Virginia. Mill House Farm was sold for £3,000 and the Simms family emigrated in 1952. When they left, Frank Newlove, his aunt and Peter Simms's cat Whisky remained behind. The Round House continued to be lived in until May 1958 when it was sold to developers R. Green, because Portslade Council was about to serve a compulsory purchase order on the house. R. Green Properties then proceeded to build twenty-six or twenty-eight houses on the land. While the building work was going ahead Green's used the Round House as an estate office.

Elsie Peirce

Working at Ronuk

Elsie Saunders was born in 1906. Aged fourteen she left school, and started in her first job straight away. Although she lived in Brighton, she came to work in Portslade because there were more jobs available there. There were several firms employing a large workforce including Flynn's Laundry, Greenfield's Laundry, the Metal Box Co. and Ronuk (maker of the famous polishes). Out of these Ronuk was considered the best firm to work for, and it was quite a feather in the cap to be employed there. When she went for her interview at Ronuk, her mother accompanied her.

In those days the big shots at the factory were Mr Fowler and Mr Felton, while Mr Brown was the works manager. Elsie described Mr Fowler as over 6ft tall and a gentleman from top to toe.

Elsie worked an 8-hour day that began promptly at 7.50 a.m. This was the starting time for girls – the boys clocked on at 8 a.m. There was no such thing as a canteen and the staff were obliged to bring in their own food, which was eaten in a small room – one for the boys and the other for the girls. There was a little gas oven, but not much else. Coffee breaks – or elevenses – were unheard of but if you felt peckish you were allowed to eat something while still at your workbench. Of course, there was no opportunity to wash your hands beforehand, and so it was a quick wipe down your overalls before taking a bite – hence the saying popular at the factory 'a mouthful of bread and a mouthful of Ronuk'.

The factory legend was that Ronuk polish had been invented by Mr Fowler's mother in her house near Holland Road Halt, Hove. Later on, Ronuk was important enough to have its own railway sidings at Portslade, and the metal sheets for the Metal Box factory were also off-loaded there – Metal Box made the tins for Ronuk. When the tins arrived at Ronuk, the first job was to knock them briskly to remove the lids, which were stored separately.

The tins came in different sizes – very large ones for industrial use, the standard size selling for 1s 9d, the small size selling for 6½d and the tiny sample tin around the size of a penny. The tins were laid out along a bench and along came a man bearing a large jug (a bit like an urn) full of molten red polish, turning the brass tap on and off and pouring the required amount into each tin. By the end of the day the men

A Ronuk advertisement from 1926. (Author)

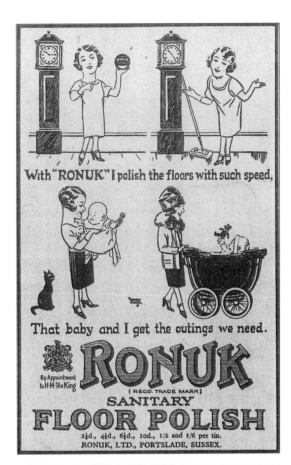

Staff of the Filling Department of Ronuk, c. 1916. Back row, left to right: George Skinner, Bert Short, Jack Smith, Fred Peirce, Fred Parsons, Arthur Packham, Fred Twine, Reg Scutt and Cyril Brenchley. Middle row: Chris Holland, Elsie Saunders, Emmie Packham, Mr Knight the foreman, Ivy Priestly and Archie Paris. Front row: Ernie Trussler, Frank Bernard and Vic Terry. Later on Elsie Saunders married Fred Peirce and Emmie married Cyril Brenchley. (Peirce)

Elsie Saunders hard at work watched by the Duke and Duchess of York, 17 October 1924. (Peirce)

who performed this task were practically reeling from inhaling the fumes of the potent mix, which included turpentine and beeswax. Conditions improved when automation was introduced and tins were filled on a conveyor belt.

Elsie once worked in the shop where lids were put on the tins. She said the girls worked like greased lightning. They kept a nest of lids under one arm and whipped them on as the tins passed by in front of them. A little man by the name of Johnnie Page used to keep an eye on this operation, and if one of the girls missed her aim and the lid dented the smooth surface of the set polish, the tin was removed from the production line, scraped out and re-filled.

The red polish was the company's most popular product. A new line was tried while Elsie worked there and she remembered filling some of the first containers. The product was a cream polish sold in small blue jars, but it never really took off, and neither did the experimental shoe blacking.

There was a great sense of excitement at Ronuk on 17 October 1924 when the Duke and Duchess of York (later King George VI and Queen Elizabeth) came on a visit. The walls adjacent to where the royal couple would walk were given a fresh coat of paint – but only half-way up – mustn't be too extravagant. Then the gardener appeared with masses of fresh cut flowers, which he solemnly proceeded to push into the earth. It is to be hoped they did not start to wilt until after the great event. Elsie was busy at her workbench as the Duke and Duchess came by and they stopped to watch her work – she kept a souvenir photograph of the occasion. Afterwards the staff were given a half-day holiday and there was a party at the Ralli Hall, Hove. It was a day long to be remembered.

Ronuk provided the girls who travelled in from Brighton with a quarterly season ticket costing 13*s*. The train drivers came to know the Ronuk girls so well that they would sometimes hold up the train until they were all aboard. The girls used to see the train crossing the Lewes Road viaduct and know it was time to start running, but the train would wait for them. It was the same story on the journey home when the girls swapped trains at Brighton station. The driver would lean out of his cab and ask, 'Where are the Ronuk girls?' During the General Strike of 1926 there were no trains, and so Ronuk sent a van to Seven Dials to pick up their staff, but it was still a long walk for some of them. Rather meanly, Ronuk did not extend the same courtesy to their homeward journey and employees were expected to find their own way home. On one occasion the girls walked to the Old Shoreham Road and hitched a lift on a passing hay-cart.

When Elsie started work at Ronuk she earned 14*s* 8*d* a week. The factory closed for a week at the beginning of August so that everyone could have a holiday – unpaid of course. This was standard treatment at the time, but Ronuk was

One of Ronuk's packing rooms, c. 1926. (Brighton & Hove Libraries)

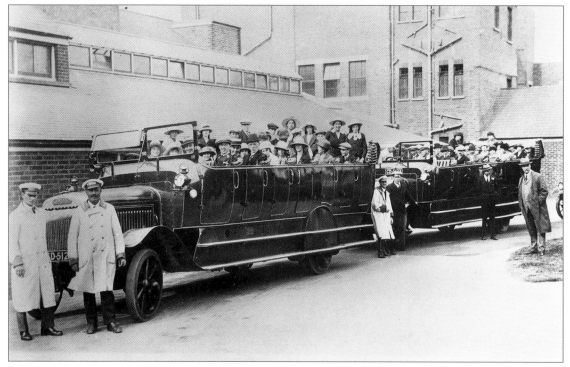

The Ronuk outing to Hastings, 1925. T. Horace Fowler, founder and managing director, stands on the right. (Peirce)

enlightened in other ways. For example, they laid on charabanc excursions for their staff, visiting places such as the Isle of Wight. The trips were greatly appreciated and many a factory romance started on the charabanc outing!

Ronuk also provided a full social life and there was some activity every weekday evening. There were stoolball and tennis, while Miss Lawrence, who worked in the office in the daytime, taught ballet. There was access to a gym as well. A splendid new Ronuk Hall was opened in the 1920s, which was used for social activities as well as being the venue for the works canteen. Ronuk's nightlife was a great bonus and Elsie and her friends joined in whole-heartedly. In fact, her father would grumble sometimes because she spent so little time at home. After arriving home from work, she would grab a quick bite to eat, change her clothes and then dash off back to Ronuk. Her father called it 'a quick run round the table'.

Elsie met her future husband on her second day at Ronuk. It so happened that she was reading a book on the train and sailed past Portslade station without noticing. She was obliged to get off at Fishersgate Halt instead. She had no idea where she was and asked some young men nearby if they knew where 'the Ronuk' was. They laughed and said they were going that way themselves. Off they went together and on the way stopped at a house to collect Fred Peirce. As Elsie was only fourteen at the time, she and Fred did not start courting until she was seventeen. The romance began after a Ronuk charabanc outing, naturally. Elsie was very patient and waited until she was twenty-four before getting married. The reason was that Fred had another love in his life – music. He spent hours practising the violin and some of his Ronuk wages went on paying for violin lessons from Miss Purdy, who lived at Southwick and taught at Lancing College. Fred worked hard at his studies and passed all his exams, which he took at Lyon & Hall's premises in Western Road, Brighton.

Ernie Harrison, who was a piano tuner at Portslade, formed a band and Fred Peirce and Reg Scutt (both Ronuk boys) and Arthur Steele joined him. They used to play at 6*d* hops in Portslade at venues such as the old church hall in Abinger Road. At length Mr Brown called Fred into his office and said bluntly, 'I think you're burning the candle at both ends,' and of course he was – working all day and playing in a band at night. Fred had worked at Ronuk for nine years and Elsie for seven when they left. But their story had a happy ending, because Fred became a success in the music world, playing with all the big bands in large ballrooms up and down the country. He even played at the Albert Hall. Elsie accompanied him on his travels.

8

Gladys Banfield

From Inskipp's
to the Wonder of Woolies

You could say that Gladys and George are Portsladian by adoption, because by 1990 they had lived in the town for over sixty years. George Ellis and Gladys Banfield are brother and sister and they have always got on well. But this chapter concentrates on Gladys's story – simply because I interviewed her first – and anyway, ladies first.

They were born in Portsmouth, Gladys arriving in 1913 and George four years after. Mrs Ellis was thirty-nine years old when Gladys was born. She had married a man two years younger than she was – thus beginning a family tradition, because both Gladys and her own daughter chose to marry younger men as well.

Mrs Ellis was a resourceful woman and remarkably independent for her time. She started work at twelve years of age and managed to save enough money to purchase two properties; one she rented out and in the other one she ran her own business. It sounds ideal – the only trouble was that her tenant was a cabinet-maker who was often behind with the rent. Sometimes he used to pay her in kind by making her a piece of furniture. She was in no rush to get married and waited until she was thirty-four before tying the knot. When George was born she sold her business.

Mr Ellis was a torpedo instructor at HMS *Vernon*. He was due to retire on pension, but the First World War intervened and he remained in the Navy until 1919. When he left the Navy he found it very difficult to find a job, but eventually he joined the Coastguard. However, it was not all plain sailing, as he was obliged to serve for a year in southern Ireland with the 'Troubles' going on all around him. He went because he had been promised a home posting after his year in Ireland.

Meanwhile, Mrs Ellis and her two children stayed behind. Mrs Ellis bought a boarding house in Southsea and took in paying guests. The family were reunited when Mr Ellis was posted to Rye Harbour, where he remained from 1922 to 1924. It was impossible to stay any longer – what with the 'Geddes axe' and the prospect of reduced pay. It was time to move on again. By this time Mrs Ellis had regained her taste for running her own business, and before her husband had finished his duties at Rye, she and George had moved to Portslade, where a small shop was

St Nicolas's Sports Team, winners of the Portslade Challenge Shield, 1927. Gladys Ellis is in the back row, second from left, between Edna and Elsie – she can't remember their surnames. The other two girls are Phyllis Terry and Lily Peacock. Middle row, left to right: Cathy Eastwood, Marie Miles (whose uncle founded the aviation firm), Mrs Mary Florence Sayers (headmistress), Mrs Kate Kenward, Bertha Hallett and Rene Bridle. Front row: Norah Barnes and Joan Adams. H.W. Tubbs of Station Road took the photograph. (Banfield)

purchased at the corner of Wolseley Road and Park Crescent. Gladys arrived with the furniture later, and Mr Ellis came last of all. Naturally, the family lived over the shop, which was a small general store. By 1927 all four of them had moved to 83 Mile Oak Road, and there the family finally settled.

Gladys attended St Nicolas's Girls' School where she enjoyed sport and was in the school athletic team. She loved playing stoolball and was disappointed when she was unable to continue playing after she left school. However, she did manage to keep up some sporting interests by going to the gym situated at the back of the Southern Cross Mission in Trafalgar Road. Here she could swing Indian clubs with the best of them, as well as leaping over the vaulting horse.

Gladys left school at the age of fourteen and took a job at Inskipp's, the draper's shop at 80 Trafalgar Road, on the corner of Bampfield Street. This shop sold everything in the clothing line from corsets and stockings to hats. Mrs Inskipp owned the shop and she was a widow with a son to bring up. She was as thin as a reed and liked to dye her hair black. Obviously she had to be careful with the pennies – no credit was permitted – but it was not much fun for Gladys, as the shop was always dark and cold in order to save on fuel and lighting. Elsie Peirce said the shop was as dark as Newgate's locker. Incidentally, while working in the shop Gladys heard women gossiping about Fred Peirce turning professional in the music world and leaving his safe job at Ronuk. They wondered if he was doing the right thing.

But to return to Inskipp's. Another reason for not having heating in the shop was because it would steam up the windows. Cold winters were common then and poor Gladys used to suffer from terrible chilblains on her feet and ankles. They were very painful and so bad they left scars. She used to buy a Snowfire block from the chemist and soften it in her hands before rubbing it on to her chilblains for a little relief. It seems chilblains were a common affliction in those days. An old-fashioned remedy was to get a bladder of lard from the butcher, work some camphor into it, and apply to the chilblains.

Gladys earned 5s a week at Inskipp's and the hours were long – from 9 a.m. to 8 p.m. on weekdays and closing time was 9 p.m. on Saturdays. Wednesday was the high spot of the week because it was a half-day. However, whichever way you look at it, she still worked a 55-hour week. She used to go home at lunchtime, and when the family moved to Mile Oak Road, George would often give her a lift back to work in the large basket of his trade bike.

One of Gladys's tasks was to sew price tags on to garments. It was not as simple as it sounds because the cotton had to go back and forth through the material with a knot at each side in just the right manner. But there was a bonus at Christmas time when she was allowed to choose any garment she might fancy in the shop. Usually her tastes ran to something practical and warm – such as a cardigan.

After Gladys had worked at Inskipp's for three or four years, she felt like a change of scene. She was aged about eighteen at the time. But her next choice was an unhappy one, so she only stayed for a short time. It was a job in a sweet shop at the corner of Portland Road, Hove.

Her next job was at Joymanco, the gas appliance manufacturer in Cambridge Grove, Hove. It was an interesting site because it was here that some of the early silent films had been made and the legend 'Kinemacolour' can still be seen from the railway, painted on the wall. There was a pleasant house (used for offices) with a double pink may tree in the garden. Gladys worked on the sewing machines, stitching leather diaphragms on to a round wire, which were later dipped into oil and graphite to become one of the components of a gas meter. While Joymanco's was not dark or cold, it was certainly noisy, and the banging of the metal workers flattening lengths of wire used to leave her ears buzzing. But she stuck it for five years until the end of 1934. Then it was a case of being pushed, rather than leaving voluntarily, as she was laid off.

Her next job was in Woolworth's, Worthing, and she cycled there and back every day. If the weather was very bad, she took a train instead (1s return to Portslade) but that was not often. She loved working at Woolies, and she reckons it was the best job she ever had. Moreover, she earned a man's wage of £2 5s a week. She worked in the

The wedding day of Vic Banfield and Gladys Ellis, 31 July 1937. Ron Coleman, Vic's brother-in-law and best man, stands on the right. The bride's parents, Edwin and Louisa Ellis, stand next to her. In the background can be glimpsed a mahogany-built railway carriage used for storage. (Banfield)

china department and later in the gardening section selling bulbs – she enjoyed both. Another bonus was being able to buy a good dinner in the staff canteen for 6*d*.

In July 1937 Gladys married Vic Banfield at St Nicolas's Church, Portslade. She wore a fetching blue outfit with pink buttons and carried a bouquet of pink carnations. On her head she wore an attractive halo hat.

Her husband was only aged twenty-one, but you could say he was old beyond his years – he had to be. His father Harry Banfield was a somewhat feckless character and a cowman by trade. Everything was fine when he was sober, but every couple of years he would go on a bender and forget about the poor cows altogether. The enraged farmer would then throw the family out of their tied cottage and they would have to start afresh somewhere else. At the time Vic and Gladys married, Harry was working away from Portslade. Life had been tough for Vic's mother too, especially since she had been crippled with arthritis ever since Vic was about four years old.

Vic's mother was a member of the Stallabrass family, and her uncle Dennis Stallabrass was famous in local annals as being the first motor car owner in Portslade in the 1890s – it was a Daimler Benz dogcart. There is an amusing anecdote about this vehicle related to me by John Broomfield. The story goes that one day Dennis met the postman in the village and offered to give him a lift up the hill. 'No thanks,' replied the postman, 'I'm in a hurry!'

Dennis Stallabrass in his Daimler Benz dogcart in Station Road (later Boundary Road) in the 1890s. (Banfield)

Vic's grandmother, Marianne Stallabrass, had arrived in Portslade from Hertford in the 1890s. She had taken the step of leaving her husband – a course of action not undertaken lightly in Victorian times – accompanied by her three children. She bought and managed Portslade Farm and died in 1908 at the age of sixty-one.

Vic's great-grandparents had their share of tragedy. They were first cousins, and although they produced seven or eight children, every other one was born stone-deaf. The mother believed that her last-born youngest son was all right, but when she learned that he too was deaf, she gave up hope and died shortly afterwards. One of the deaf sons managed to find a job tending the plants in the Camellia House at Harrods.

The Stallabrass family lived in a charming house at Portslade called Hill Brow initially, but changed to Milestones later. It was built in the colonial style with verandas around the house from which there were marvellous views. There were four bedrooms, a dining room, a drawing room and a bathroom with hot and cold running water, and the house was advertised for sale shortly after Marianne Stallabrass died. The house stood in grounds of 7 acres and the freehold was priced at £2,950. The advert also stated that the family might be willing to sell the house on its own with half an acre of ground for £1,300. The house was later demolished when Rowan Close was built on the site and on the surrounding land in about 1961.

Meanwhile, we have rather lost sight of Vic Banfield. He married at a young age, it is true, but he also started building up his own business at a tender age as well.

When he was seventeen he purchased an old model-T Ford for £5 and embarked upon a career as a haulage contractor. He would transport practically anything anywhere. Gladys remembers him as a very hard worker and a good provider – when he was not at work, he would be busy improving the home. Incidentally, their home was a brand-new house in Brasslands Drive (a road named appropriately enough after the Stallabrass family) that cost all of £590. Vic celebrated their marriage by buying an Austin 7 tourer (or Chummy as Gladys calls it), and they enjoyed many trips in it.

Gladys remembers well the Sunday war was declared, 3 September 1939. It was a glorious sunny day and their firstborn son, called Carol Edwin, was out in the garden in his pram. Then the sirens went off and Gladys got all het up thinking of the baby's safety, but Vic kept saying, 'Don't worry, it'll be all right'. In fact, his call-up papers were deferred for a year because he was running his own business. But he was obliged to join up when his son was a year old.

He joined the 7th Surrey Regiment and served for six years. Before he left he gave Gladys a nest egg of £100 in notes. She racked her brains to think of a safe hiding place, and eventually hit on the idea of putting the roll of notes in a tin and placing the tin in the oven. Of course you can imagine what happened, but fortunately it was not a total disaster. Think of a Triplex grate – an old-fashioned range in fact – with two trivets and the oven at the top. It was here Gladys hid her tin. Then a friend's husband came home on leave and they both came to tea. She lit the fire and they enjoyed a good gossip over a cup of tea. When the subject turned to money

A trade card advertising Portslade Farm. (Banfield)

Hill Brow, later called Milestones, c. 1908. (Banfield)

Gladys suddenly leapt out of her chair like a scalded cat. She retrieved the tin in the nick of time as the notes were already steaming.

Gladys and Vic's second son, Ashley, was born in December 1944 – exactly nine months after Vic had come home for D-Day embarkation leave. The baby arrived safely at home in Brasslands Drive and there were no complications. Vic was fortunate in being able to see his new son when the baby was still only a month old as his regiment had drawn lots to see who should go home on leave, and Vic's ticket came up. Some of the officers proffered good cash offers for the ticket but Vic was not to be tempted as he was too anxious to get home.

Gladys's last excursion into motherhood was not until 1955 when Melanie Marianne was born at Southlands Hospital. She was a lucky little girl, because not only did she have doting parents, but two brothers who were old enough to be tickled pink at the prospect of having a baby sister in the family.

After Vic left the Army he started to build up his haulage business again. The first step was to buy an old Dodge, which he put to rights with the help of his brother-in-law, George Ellis. Eventually, Carol came into the business, and so there were two lorries driving about Portslade painted in Cambridge blue. Gladys also lent a hand by taking the phone calls and the bookings. Vic died in 1981. In 2004 Gladys celebrated her ninety-first birthday.

9

George Ellis

Butcher's Boy, Baker's Roundsman and More

George Ellis was born in Portsmouth in 1909. He came to Portslade in 1924. When he was fifteen he went to work for Frank Hart, butcher, at 88 Trafalgar Road, Portslade. He earned 10s a week. Later his wages rose to 17s 6d, a week and eventually to £1 10s. Out of his pay he had to buy his own striped apron and overalls for shop use. Mrs Wicks owned no. 88. She was the widow of a master builder and speculator who had built houses in Trafalgar Road with Tudor-style gables. There was an underground meat vault where the temperature was always cool – even in hot weather.

George hoped to make his way in the world more profitably, and so with this in mind he left Hart's in 1931 and took a similar post in Hobden's, a butcher in Victoria Terrace on Hove seafront. The pay was around the same but the tips and Christmas box were better. You can still see the decorative blue-glazed tiles there that adorned Hobden's shop.

In 1935 Leslie Garrard, one of the men employed at Hart's, left for a post in a new shop in Elm Drive, Hove. Mr Hart then offered George the job at £2 a week. Of course, George jumped at the chance. At that time Hart's was a thriving business employing six men and a boy. The staff consisted of George Ellis and his father, Frank Hart and his sons Reuben and Bert, Bill Brotherhood and the boy Fred Smith. The shop sold English meat and plenty of locally caught rabbits.

One Good Friday George nearly lost two fingers. The pious might comment that he should not have been working on such a sacred day. The shop was not open to the public and the blinds were drawn down, but there were many joints to be trimmed and prepared for the weekend. George put his fingers under a lump of suet to cut off the required amount and he brought his knife down through the lot of them, but fortunately not right through the bones.

By this time George had a steady girlfriend. Or to use the parlance of the time, he had been walking out with Ellen Licence since 1932 when he was twenty-three and she was sweet sixteen. He had first set eyes on her when she was a twelve-year-old schoolgirl. However, before a wedding could be contemplated there was the knotty

Frank Hart's shop at 88 Trafalgar Road, c. 1926. Left to right: Frank Hart, George Ellis, Reuben Hart and Leslie Garrard. (Ellis)

problem of lack of money to solve. When George approached Reuben Hart about the matter, he was told that if he were to be given a pay rise it would mean that Mr Ellis senior would have to be made redundant. So George had no option but to search for a better paid job.

Circumstances improved in 1938 when George got a new job at £2 5s a week plus commission and Fred Godfray lent him an old Austin 7 tourer, a four-seater. The car had a leatherised roof that had rotted in places, and so Fred purchased a nice piece of canvas, which he secured with bulldog clips. Seat covers were run up from old curtain material. In this resplendent vehicle, plus a 5-gallon drum of oil, George and Ellen drove to Clacton for a belated honeymoon. Later on the same car was sold to Vic Banfield.

George's new job was driving the van for Gigin's Bakery, whose premises were on the corner of Franklin Road and Station Road, Portslade. It is somewhat ironic that with his love of engines and his long-standing ambition to be a motor mechanic, George should have landed a job where the horsepower was literally a horse! Gigin's kept a stable of eight horses at the back of the bakery, and a Welsh ostler by the name of Pugh looked after them. George had no experience in handling horses, so he was accompanied for the first three or four days – then he was left to his own devices. Fortunately, the horse was a sensible creature, and as his name was Colonel it was obvious who was boss.

It was a large round. George and Colonel ventured out in the early morning with the van full of loaves of bread, cakes and 'sundries' – commission could be earned on the latter two. The van also had to accommodate Colonel's nosebag, plus a foot brake and slipper for coping with animals and vehicle on steep, slippery hills. From the stables in Franklin Road, the pair made their way along New Church Road to the Belfast pub in Belfast Street, where there was a large standing order. The route continued along Blatchington Road to Lansdowne Road, turned up York Avenue to Davigdor Road and the final lap on to the Seven Dials, Montpelier Road, Upper North Street and Dyke Road, calling at various houses on the way. On one occasion when George parked the van in Clifton Terrace for longer than usual, Colonel became bored, and despite the brake being on, managed to drag the van half-way up Dyke Road by the time George caught up with him.

Colonel certainly was a character. George remembered another occasion when he was putting on the harness first thing in the morning. He was in the act of drawing up the belly strap when Colonel turned his head and gave George's arm a playful nip. It might have been amusing for Colonel, but it left George with a nasty bruise. He had some trouble with Colonel's mouth another time. They were out on their rounds when a lady warned her children to keep away from the vicious horse. George sprang to Colonel's defence. 'He's as gentle as a lamb,' he said, stroking the horse's neck and nose. Before he knew what had happened, old Colonel had George's hand firmly in his mouth. George tried valiantly to extricate his fingers while at the same time reassuring his fascinated audience.

Colonel could be quite skittish when the mood took him. There was the memorable day in 1939 when, for some reason, the round was much

George Ellis with his wife Ellen and daughter Barbara, 1939. (Ellis)

shorter than usual. Anyway, Colonel thought he was being put back in his stables before the proper time, so he kicked up his heels and disappeared at a fast trot down Franklin Road and into Norway Street. But he only went round the block, and soon reappeared at the stables, well pleased with his adventure.

1938 was an important year for the Ellis family. In September George was on his rounds when he saw his wife Ellen and his sister Gladys walking along Clifton Terrace, carrying a small case. It took him some moments to realise they were on their way to the Maternity Hospital in Buckingham Road. Ellen had a daughter, Barbara. Their second child, a boy called Colin, was born in 1946. Ellen's labour pains started while Gladys was having a night out at the pictures, but sensibly she waited until Gladys got home before getting on with things.

Christmas 1938 stood out in George's memory. It had snowed and was bitterly cold. He and Colonel were out on their round from 7 a.m. to 8 p.m. Coming home along New Church Road, George felt frozen to the marrow. To try and boost his circulation, he climbed down from the van and ran beside Colonel. Apparently, the old wooden blocks used to line the road were prone to the frost, thus making the going much colder.

During the Second World War George joined the 10th Army Field Workshop, which was stationed at the Brewery in Portslade Village. George was officially billeted, which meant he was paid 6*d* a night for the pleasure of sleeping in his own bed. He had an idea that he might make contact with men in the motor trade, and eventually realised his ambition of becoming a motor mechanic. After all, the man in charge of the outfit was Captain Caffyn (later promoted to Brigadier), whose family owned Caffyn's Garage. George's comfortable arrangements ceased in March 1940 when his unit was shipped to France aboard the screw ferry *Ben Macree*. Major Caffyn came into his own in France during the Dunkirk evacuation, as he knew the French roads well from his peacetime travels in the area. He was able to get his men to Brest in safety with the loss of only one of three recovery units – but it was a near run thing.

George saw a great deal of the world during his war service. Besides his brief visit to France and a longer spell in Scotland, he was also in Egypt, North Africa, Syria (with some leave spent in Beirut), Palestine, Sicily and Italy. Eventually he returned home safe and sound and kept going until well into his eighties.

10

Miss Austen

A Teacher's Life

Although Gladys Austen had a long association with Portslade schools, she was not a native of Sussex. She was born in West Hartlepool in 1886. She might have stayed there all her life had not her father fallen ill and the family moved south in search of a kinder climate. In about 1900 they settled at Portslade in Station Road and later moved to 27 Boundary Road, Hove, which was later occupied by a business that sold homemade ice cream. Mr Austen had been a school inspector for schools in the north of England, and when they moved south he became clerk to Portslade Urban District Council. It is not surprising that Gladys and her sister Agnes (a third sister died in childhood) should chose to follow a career in education. Gladys Austen's first teaching post was at Wick, near Littlehampton, and she became a teacher at St Nicolas's School, Portslade, in 1912. She was then a young woman of twenty-six. Also on the staff was Arthur Gates, who had joined the school in 1908.

In August 1914 Arthur joined the Territorials, and it was not long before he was called up. Meanwhile, Gladys continued to teach; she was on friendly terms with the Gates family, particularly Emma with whom she sometimes played cards. She kept a diary, which she wrote in pencil in a hardback 'Ladies Year Book', printed with recipes and useful tips for the garden at the foot of every page. Her jottings for the year 1917 provide an insight into the type of life she led. She was an energetic young woman who enjoyed long walks and bicycle rides. She loved going to the Theatre Royal or on to the pier to listen to the band. On New Year's Day she went to the pantomime *Aladdin*, courtesy of her uncle, and afterwards they had tea at Lyon's Corner House. In February she saw D'Oyley Carte's production of *The Mikado* and her favourite songs were 'Flowers that Bloom in the Spring' and 'Tit Willow'. On leaving the Theatre Royal to catch the bus home, she found that it was full, and without turning a hair she walked all the way to Boundary Road.

Gladys enjoyed sketching and reading, and was often to be found playing a game of whist with her friends. She became an enthusiastic gardener, which stood the family in good stead when vegetables became scarce during the First World War, and indeed she recorded that sometimes it was impossible to buy potatoes in the shops. On Sundays she went to church twice. She obviously liked to ring the changes, since she attended

2nd Lieutenant Arthur Gates looking fit and strong, but he only survived the war by seven years. (Gedye)

the morning service at St Andrew's, Portslade, while in the afternoon she often went to St Philip's. She became a connoisseur of sermons and made notes on their content and the preacher's text. It appears that the clergymen were quite caught up in the war effort, and urged their parishioners to purchase war bonds, while at the same time cultivating frugal habits. The reality of war was brought home to her when she saw a horrible incident. On 22 May 1917 two British aeroplanes collided – one fell into Aldrington Recreation Ground (Wish Park) and the other on to the beach. One of the pilots was 2nd Lieutenant Crapp, who was buried on the west side of St Leonard's Churchyard, near the wall. Gladys reported that hundreds of sightseers gathered and many carried off pieces of aircraft as souvenirs (see page 62).

Twice during the same month she watched the searchlight operating from Brooker Hall (Hove Museum). On 11 May the searchlight located a plane in its beam, and the plane set off two star shells, one red and one green. In February she reported that the Gas Works steamer *John Miles* had been torpedoed near Hartlepool. In August she saw a party of German PoWs at work in a field under the charge of a British soldier, who stood with fixed bayonet. She went to visit wounded soldiers in Brighton Hospital (renamed the Kitchener Hospital) and made up parcels to send to the soldiers at the Front. In May 1917 Arthur Gates came home on leave and visited St Nicolas's School.

School work continued much as usual. In February Gladys was busy picking out the three best essays on thrift for the competition set by the Mayor. In the same month her colleague, Mrs Atherfold, told her all about an argument with headmaster Mr Price about school-closing time. She too had experienced ups and downs with Mr Price. In June she cycled to Black Rock to collect samples of seaweed for her lessons the next day. Earlier in the year she was somewhat embarrassed when the mother of one of her 'boys' asked for a loan of 2*s*. She had to refuse gently but firmly. Usually she went home to lunch, but if it was pouring with rain, she stayed at school. In February school was closed for a while because it was impossible to buy coal for heating – it was a very cold winter that year.

Family legend has it that when Arthur was demobbed, he had a quiet word with his mother to find out if Gladys had got engaged while he had been away.

His mother replied, 'No, not yet, but you had better get a move on!' Arthur and Gladys married in January 1921. By then Gladys had been teaching at St Nicolas's School for nine years. She was presented with a set of fish knives as a wedding present. Arthur could have returned to his old job at the school, as the position was kept open for him, but his war experiences had unsettled him and he decided to take a post in Cologne, Germany. However, when Gladys became pregnant, they returned to England and moved into 45 Boundary Road, Hove, not far away from the Austen household. In 1922 Muriel was born – Gladys being thirty-five years old at the time. Meanwhile, Arthur took a post at St Andrew's School, Wellington Road, Portslade. He taught the boys woodwork and enjoyed woodcarving as a hobby. He carved several hymn boards for local churches and inscribed the names of Old Boys on the backs of chairs in Lancing College Chapel. Another piece of work of his was a beautifully cut Latin motto – *Deliberandum est diu quod statuendum est semel* – Deliberate often, decide once. He also enjoyed playing the violin and harp.

Miss Gladys Austen with her class of boys at St Nicolas's School, c. 1920. Back row, left to right: Ernest Chadwick, George Kelsey, Ernie Redman, Dick Robinson, -?-, -?-, Charlie Hickling, Horace Candy and Fred Mack. Middle row: William Broomfield, two Stephen brothers, Harold Ridley, Fred Hilton, Archie Greenyer, -?-. Front row: Ernie Hills, Charlie Pullen, Fred Nicholas, Charlie Stanford, Reg Walls and George Clevett. (Greenyer)

In 1924 their second child, Don, was born. However, in the following year tragedy struck. Arthur went down with pnuemonia and he did not respond to treatment. He died on 30 November 1925. Three months after his death their third child, Graham, was born. There were no Government handouts in those days, and so Gladys had no option but to resume full-time work in order to provide for her children. She took a post at her old school, St Andrew's, while a succession of paid helps looked after the children. Most were kind-hearted but one was sent packing for cruelty.

As soon as school age was reached, which for Don happened in 1929, Aunt Agnes took a hand. By then Agnes Austen was acting head of Connaught Road Infants' School, and Don accompanied her there every morning on the bus, fare 1*d*. Don continued his education at the Ellen Street School, then Connaught Road Seniors, finishing with a scholarship to Brighton, Hove and Sussex Grammar School. Meanwhile, Gladys continued to teach at St Andrew's until she retired. She died in 1971 aged eighty-four.

11

The Tate Family

The name of Tate is a familiar one in Sussex because of a string of garages, filling stations and the new addition – a garden centre at Newhaven. It is interesting to note that the family's fortunes were founded at Portslade. In the 1990s Jonathan Tate ran the family firm, but to trace the beginnings we need to go back to his great-grandfather, Alfred Tate, who had a great interest in motor cars.

The famous Emancipation Run of 1896 from London to Brighton celebrated the end of a law which stated that all motor vehicles must be preceded by a man waving a red flag. Alfred Tate had once been the bearer of a red flag, while his friend Albert Dudeney remembered conducting a steamroller through the streets of Brighton without realising until later that the driver was roaring drunk.

Alfred Tate took part in the Emancipation Run. Unhappily, his Daimler overturned at Handcross, so he never had the pleasure of a triumphant arrival at Brighton. But he turned the situation to his advantage by having the vehicle towed back to his workshop, where he converted it into a van – in fact the first commercial vehicle in the area. It was hardly a sophisticated conversion because he merely cobbled together the body and tilt of an ordinary horse-drawn cart, and attached them to where the back part of the car had been. Motoring in those early days was pretty much a hit and miss affair anyway. For instance, the Tates never went motoring without a trusty bag of French nails, which were used to hammer back the solid tyres, should they come adrift.

It was not long before the Tates gained a reputation for being rather good at tinkering with motorcar engines. So soon other car owners brought their vehicles for attention. Thus it was that a small engineering works grew up at the back of Tate's Laundry on the north-east corner of Foredown Drive. It was a somewhat odd combination to have the engines, dirt and oil right next door to the laundry, which boasted of having the finest drying grounds in the south. Until the arrival of the Daimler van the laundry's collection and delivery service was carried out by horse and cart.

This part of Portslade became quite a Tate enclave; Alfred Tate built himself a house (now 206 Old Shoreham Road), his brother-in-law lived next door at no. 208 and his son Fred lived at no. 210. Later on, Alfred's son Albert lived with his family at 1 Benfield Way, which was where John Tate was born in 1930. The stables occupied by the laundry delivery horses were at the back of no. 208, and alongside was an underground tank holding 300 gallons of petrol. When the tank was installed

*Alfred Tate's Daimler, registration no. AP 23, took part in the Emancipation Run of 1896.
(Tate)*

this was considered a huge amount of petrol. The petrol was cranked up by hand, and of course, you only took one gallon on board with each winding of the pump.

Alfred Tate had yet another string to his bow – he owned the Majestic cinema in Edward Street, Brighton, which was managed by Lyndsay, his third son. Alfred's granddaughter remembered going to watch Pearl White in the silent movies put on there.

The films were changed weekly, with new films arriving by train. However, in 1919 there was a train strike. This caused consternation among local cinema managers, because how were they going to receive their new films? Albert and Fred decided to take the laundry van up to the London distribution centre. It was a long drive, and not without incident, but they succeeded in obtaining new films for the Majestic. When other cinema owners heard about the excursion, they asked if Tate's would change their films as well. The enterprise grew to such an extent that Tate's were collecting and supplying films to over thirty cinemas in the area. The service lasted for fifty-nine years until the decline of the cinema trade and difficulties at the London distribution centre made the business more trouble than it was worth.

In 1929 the Tates opened their first garage at Southern Cross. There were two hand-operated pumps, serving petrol at the pavement, and a large advertisement for Shell petrol.

The Tates have had their fair share of fires and natural disasters. The laundry building burned down in 1954, and in 1971 there was a spectacular fire at their garage at the foot of Applesham Way – owned by the Tates, but rented to Evans Halshaw. When John Tate received a phone call alerting him to the fire, he looked out of his window and saw the sky lit up and a huge pall of smoke. Then the Great Storm of October 1987 smashed every greenhouse set out in their large display area south of the Old Shoreham Road, while the wall of an adjoining house crashed through their car showroom, demolishing several brand-new cars. Altogether, their businesses throughout Sussex suffered £250,000 in damage in the storm. John Tate, who by then had retired from the firm, was landed with the complicated task of compiling the various insurance claims.

John Tate remembered the carefree days of riding his bicycle as a boy along the Old Shoreham Road, weaving in and out of the white lines and being quite unperturbed by the small amount of traffic. During the Second World War he and his friends used to sit in a row on top of the bank in Victoria Recreation Ground watching enemy aircraft dive-bombing ships in the harbour, which the ships sought to evade by running up their own barrage balloons.

Tate's innovative van was the first commercial vehicle in the area, 1908. Albert Tanner is the little boy on the left. (Tate)

The Tates had a long association with ships, and not just as mere spectators. For a start, Tate's invented a gun depression gear for use on the well-known Oerlikon guns mounted on so many ships of the Royal Navy. Without this device a temperamental Oerlikon could inflict more damage to the funnel of its own ship than it could on an enemy target. The gear proved to be such an invaluable device that eventually the Navy had it fitted as standard equipment.

Tate's also went into the ship repair and salvage business. Their first customer was a tanker called *Shell Brit* that was bombed on 18 November 1940 while berthed at Shell Wharf in the early part of the war. A visiting butcher's boy, William Wood, was killed in the attack. Tate's made the tanker seaworthy once more. Another vessel that stood out in memory was the French minesweeper *President Briand*, which had previously been a trawler. She was wrecked at Shoreham on a beach that had been planted with land mines as part of the anti-invasion defences. She lay there like a beached whale while people wondered what on earth to do with her. After the mines had been cleared, Tate's took her in hand. The salvage operation took many months, as there was no heavy lifting gear, and the largest lorry could only carry about 3 tons. Steamrollers were brought from Worthing, and their winches used to right the vessel gradually on the spring tides. The tug *Harold Brown* from Shoreham eventually hauled the ship off the beach.

Tate's continued to take an interest in engineering after the war by designing and manufacturing equipment for overhead power lines, which were used in this country and abroad. In 1957 this business and the premises rebuilt on the site of the old laundry were sold.

John Tate took a great interest in the local community, in which his family had been known for generations. He was much amused some years ago at being recognised as a Tate by an old blind woman who had never met him before, but who had worked for his grandfather at the laundry. Presumably his voice was similar to that of his grandfather.

John Tate was concerned about the plight of many old people living on their own in poor conditions. As a founder member and Past President of Portslade Rotary Club, he arranged a meeting with Portslade councillors and persuaded them that warden-controlled flats would be of great

Peggy Dudeney working at Tate's Laundry, c. 1909. (Brighton & Hove Libraries)

A stone laying ceremony at Windlesham Close performed by Peter Gladwin, chairman of Portslade Urban District Council, in the 1960s. John Tate stands on the right. (Author)

benefit to the town and many old people in need. The Rotary Club's Housing Association was able to build Rotary Point in Windlesham Close on land purchased from Portslade Council, while the council decided to build Evelyn Court on an adjacent site and Hazelholt in Chalky Road.

By 1990 Tate's was still a family-owned business. Jonathan Tate was assisted by his cousin Trevor Meadows who managed the garages, his wife Beverley who dealt with house plants, his sister Angela Clift who managed the large restaurant at the Newhaven Garden Centre and his sister Paula Windsor who manufactured many of the concrete garden ornaments.

12

Leslie Hamilton

Over Thirty Years a Councillor

Leslie Hamilton was born in 1918 in St Aubyns Road, Portslade, the middle of three brothers. The Hamilton family had recently moved from London to avoid the Zeppelin raids. His father had been a milkman before the war, but after Army service he worked for the bus company Thomas Tilling. For many years he was on the no. 6 route, which ran from Portslade station to Brighton station; there was a brief flirtation with no. 3 bus route and then it was back to the good old no. 6. His mother earned 8*d* an hour as a 'daily' in a large house along New Church Road.

Les was educated at the old St Andrew's School, Portslade, but after reorganisation he found himself with the rest of the senior boys at St Nicolas's School – in the building on the west side of Locks Hill. Some of the masters moved too, including Reg Broadbank and the head, Mr J.W. Burn, which was why the school earned the nickname of Burns's Academy. Mr Burn hailed from the north, and he had a dim view of the local talent. 'You boys look as intelligent as a bunch of cows,' he used to tell them before shouting at them, 'Get your books out.' But with his broad accent 'books' sounded more like 'boots' to the boys. One daring boy, all wide-eyed innocence, would ask, 'Our boots, sir?' The chemistry laboratory was one small cupboard. You opened the door, dragged out a trestle table, set up a tripod, clambered on to a chair to reach the gas bracket, stuck a tube over the outlet to connect with the Bunsen burner, scrambled off the chair and lit the gas. Needless to say, experiments were few and far between.

In the late 1920s young Les had a Saturday morning job helping the Co-op milkman, which earned him 4*d* and a large Chelsea bun hot from the bakery. In those days milk was still sold straight from the churn. It was a well-known joke that an astute milkman left the lid off the top of his churn when it rained. A favourite childhood nibble was tiger nuts, sold for 1*d* a packet. Tiger nuts (*cyperus esculantus*) or chufas were dried tubers of sedge which were about the same size as a hazelnut and tasted nutty and slightly sweet.

Hamilton left school in 1933 at the age of fourteen and went to work in the Co-op Bakery, Portland Road, where he earned 10*s* a week. His duties included greasing the bread and cake tins, cooking doughnuts in a huge vat of bubbling fat, lifting them out and inserting a dab of strawberry jam. He progressed to grander things

St Nicolas's School football team, 1932. Back row, left to right: Ray Broadbank, Joe Figgins, John Whiting and J.W. Burn (headmaster). Third row: Johnnie Meaking, Squib Nelson and Johnnie French. Second row: Bill Peters, Les Hamilton, Cyril Peters, Jackie Powell and Herbert Darling. Front row: Harold Reynolds, Horace Hamper and young Purdy. (Hamilton)

such as making slab cakes and wedding cakes. But if he wanted to stay at the bakery, he would have to start working the night shift, and as he did not fancy that he decided to switch to the Co-op butcher's instead.

In 1939 he joined Hore Belisha's Militia – all twenty-year-old lads. They were paid 1s 6d a day and the walking out dress consisted of a black jacket and flannel trousers. In October 1939 Hamilton was called up and attached to the 44th Home Counties Territorials. He was determined to marry Olive King before he was posted abroad. He had met her the previous year while dancing to music at Hove bandstand on the seafront. The couple were married at St Barnabas's Church on 3 February 1940. On his wedding day Hamilton received two telegrams, one of congratulations, the other ordering him to report back immediately. He ignored the latter. When he returned to his unit on Monday he found everything packed up for Norway. But Norway collapsed and instead the unit was sent to France. Hamilton was part of RASC (509 Company), but it was a short trip as he was soon evacuated

Les Hamilton and Olive King were married on 3 February 1940 at St Barnabas's Church, Hove. The bride's sister Mary is the bridesmaid on the left, and the bridesmaid on the right is Joyce Funnell, a cousin. The little girl is Patricia Church, Olive's niece. (Hamilton)

from Dunkirk. Another part of his war service took him to Tripoli, North Africa, where he served under General Sir Brian Robertson at HQA1.

While Les was in Tripoli he decided he wanted to enter local politics after the war. He was eventually elected as a Labour councillor to Portslade Council in 1958. By this time he was working for Co-op Insurance, and he and Olive were happily settled with three children. One of the first things to occupy his attention in 1958 was the plight of seventeen unmade roads, which included the top of Stanley Avenue, North Lane and Southdown Avenue. Developers simply built the houses and left the roads as they were. Portslade Council stepped in and made up the roads, but the cost had to be spread between the people occupying houses with frontage to the relevant roads – it worked out at £3 per foot.

Les chaired most of the major committees, and was Chairman of Portslade Council from 1964 to 1965. Portslade and Hove were amalgamated in 1974, but not altogether with the sanction of Portslade people. Indeed Portslade councillors would have preferred to join up with Southwick and Shoreham. But Hove was desperately anxious for Portslade to join it, because it hoped that with a larger combined population there was less chance of being gobbled up by Brighton. In the event it was the Boundary Commission that made the decision. Hamilton joined the new council where he was leader of the Labour opposition, consisting of himself and his son, Les Hamilton Jnr. But the Hamiltons were well respected for their hard work, even among their political opponents.

In 1978 Les was elected as Hove's first Labour Mayor. It was a remarkable decision, as there were two Tory candidates as well as an overwhelming Tory majority on the council. In 1996 he did it again. The council selection committee chose him unanimously to be Hove's last mayor before amalgamation with Brighton. The Tory nominee had been the popular Jenny Langston. In May 1994 Les was chosen to be chairman of East Sussex County Council – the first Labour chairman in its history. On 17 February 1994 Les was made a Freeman of the Borough of Hove. In April 1995 a palm tree was planted in Easthill Park to mark his long service. He finally retired from the council in April 1997 at the age of seventy-eight. By that time he and Olive had notched up fifty-seven years of marriage. In the 1998 New Year Honours' List Hamilton was awarded the OBE for his service to the community. He was very much involved in the life of Portslade, being a member of a number of local societies, as well as governor of two schools and president of Brighton District Dunkirk Veterans' Association. He died on 23 December 2000 and was given a magnificent funeral in January 2001. In the words of Adam Trimingham (*Evening Argus*, 18 January 2001):

Hundreds of people attended a highly traditional funeral last week for former Hove Mayor Leslie Hamilton at the parish church of All Saints. They ranged from the great and the good to ordinary people he had helped during the years who wanted to pay their last respects to him. The funeral was a moving occasion because Mr Hamilton was unusually well-liked right across the political spectrum and because he was a regular church-goer. All the clerics who took part in the service, from the Bishop of Chichester to the Vicar of Hove, had known him personally.

His widow received hundreds of letters of condolence.

Les Hamilton in his mayoral robes, 1978. (Hamilton)

13

Reg Forrest

A Peashooter at the Picturedrome

Reg Forrest was born at 9 St Andrew's Road, Portslade, in 1914. His father was a printer by trade, having been apprenticed to Emery's of Hove, but Army service during the war meant he was away from home a great deal, including a spell in Salonika. Reg had two vivid memories of the war years. He was playing in North Street with other children (it was a relatively safe playground from the traffic point of view then) when two British aeroplanes collided overhead and pieces of metal and scraps of fuselage clattered down on to the road all around them. One plane crashed on to Wish Park, the other on to the seashore, and both pilots were killed. One of them, 2nd Lieutenant Crapp, was buried in St Leonard's Churchyard. The accident occurred on 22 May 1917 and young Reg was only three years old. The second memory concerned Armistice Day when Reg was scared out of his wits by the explosion of fireworks and bangers let off to celebrate the event, and he bolted into a bed occupied by a kindly neighbour in the rooms they occupied in Clarendon Place.

Reg was an only child. His closest companion was little Gracie Silverthorne whose parents had a fishmonger's shop in North Street. They always went off to school together, but once they arrived they were segregated as a matter of course. After school he and Gracie came home together, and many were the occasions Reg spent in the room behind the shop eating crab claws and legs kindly supplied by Mr Silverthorne. The Silverthornes also smoked herrings for bloaters. Reg enjoyed watching Mr Silverthorne make up the fire in the huge fireplace, then cover it with oak sawdust and arrange the herrings on long rods over the heat, with a pan underneath to catch the fat.

Next door to St Andrew's School was the Star Model Laundry owned by Mr Miles. During break time the boys often sat on a wall overlooking a large garage at the back where the proprietor's son, Fred Miles, was busy building an aircraft. Although Fred helped out at the laundry, doing deliveries and so on, his heart had been set on a career in aviation ever since he was taken up for a quick flip around Shoreham Airport. Eventually, Fred's enthusiasm was to lead to the foundation of the Miles Aircraft Company.

It seemed that North Street was full of interesting characters in those days. Charlie Drew was a little chap who earned his living as a barber and hairdresser, but he did more shaving than anything else – with a cut-throat razor of course. He had the strange habit of settling his customer into the chair, lathering him up, wiping the razor up and down the strop and then disappearing for a couple of pints in the nearby Clarendon pub. As often as not the abandoned customer would grow tired of waiting and shave himself.

On the corner of Clarendon Place was a watchmaker and jeweller's shop run by Mr Skinner, who was always very polite and an excellent clock repairer. The Andrews sisters ran a newsagent's shop nearby, and their father was a stern, bearded man who terrified the children. Next door to Silverthorne's was Took's, a general ironmonger, and nearby was Still's Bakery, well known for the quality of its bread. Strangely enough the bake-house was situated underneath the shop. On the opposite corner to Camden Street was Curd the butcher, who was later killed in a motorcycle accident. Mr Owen from Wales ran a marvellous

Charles Ernest Forrest, his wife Charlotte Mary and their son Reg photographed in 1916 by H.W. Tubb. Mr Forrest wears the uniform of the Royal Garrison Artillery. (Forrest)

general store, which stocked absolutely everything, most of it hanging down from the ceiling. It was like an Aladdin's cave to the children. It was the sort of place you might find a tin bath cheek by jowl with a sack of apples.

Then there was the Picturedrome cinema. Every Saturday afternoon Reg and his friends went there – it cost 1*d* to sit downstairs and 2*d* to sit in the balcony. It was more fun being upstairs, because the boys took along their peashooters to try and hit the bald patch on top of caretaker Jess Willard's head as he patrolled the stalls downstairs. He would often look up and shake his fist at them, as they were pretty good shots. Eventually, Willard settled for a more peaceful life and became a chimney sweep. There was no such refinement as a screen at the Picturedrome – the films were projected on to a white-painted wall. But it was still a marvellous time for the children, who would be enraptured by the weekly cliff-hangers. A lighting system that gently dimmed was unheard of, and when the lights were turned off a sudden blackness ensued and the children let out a roar of anticipation. On one occasion the reel of film caught alight, but with great presence of mind the boy projectionist threw it out into the street. Mr Reynolds purchased the Picturedrome and it was converted into the Pavilion cinema. Mrs Reynolds helped out in those days of silent film by providing the music. This she did with the assistance of a radiogram-type instrument called a panatrope located in the pit, on which she would play an appropriate record. On the subject of music, Reg took piano lessons with

For a while Reg attended St Winifred's School. He is the boy wearing a dark jumper on the extreme left of the second row from the back. The field in the background is now home to St Richard's Flats. (Forrest)

Miss Earl who lived at 24 St Andrew's Road. On the north-east corner of the road lived Dr Dunker who was the family doctor. Although he was German he seems to have escaped being interned during the war.

Reg's first school was St Winifred's, a small private establishment run in St Andrew's Church Hall on the corner of St Andrew's Road, popularly known as the Scout Hut. After that he attended St Andrew's School, Portslade, which he left at the age of eleven, and East Hove Boys' School at the top of Holland Road. While he was there in about 1928 a huge fire broke out at Hannington's Depository nearby. The boys lined up in the playground enthralled by the spectacle before they were dragged reluctantly away by their teachers.

Reg left school in 1929. There was not much work about because of the depression, and when a friend invited him to come and help out at his place he jumped at the chance. The friend had a hairdressing business, and young Reg soon learned the trade, coming to the conclusion that it was not a bad way to earn a living. Eventually, he acquired his own hairdressing business at 102 Old Shoreham Road, Portslade, next door to Tate's Garage. Later, when Tate's wanted to expand, he moved along to no. 94, having a shop front installed in a private house.

But before the move the Second World War intervened. Reg was exempt from call-up for a year because he was running his own business. But he decided to volunteer for the RAF, and went to a large house in Eaton Road for training sessions, where he learned telegraphy and Morse code. When he received call-up papers from the Army, he showed them to his RAF officer who said, 'They can't have you, you're one of us', and back the papers went with a full explanation. This happened twice. In 1942 he and his wife Gwendoline were celebrating their first Christmas as a married couple. On Christmas Day as they were about to sit down to dinner, there was a knock at the front door and there stood a plain-clothes policeman. He wanted Reg to come along to the police station in St Andrew's Road to see the superintendent, but fortunately he was allowed to eat his dinner first. The superintendent was an old acquaintance, as he used to enjoy a pint with Reg's father. However, this was not to young Reg's advantage, as his father was soon informed of any misdemeanour. This time the superintendent had in his hand a warrant to arrest Reg as an Army deserter. Reg explained the complicated situation and the super-intendent accepted it. Reg rather wanted to keep the warrant as a souvenir, as it was a handsome document adorned with a red seal. But of course that was not allowed – it had to be returned through official channels accompanied by the correct forms to be formally destroyed. Reg went on to join the RAF and spent his war service doing hush-hush work he was not allowed to divulge to anyone. If friends were curious, it was all right to let them think it was radar, which was just coming in. But it was not.

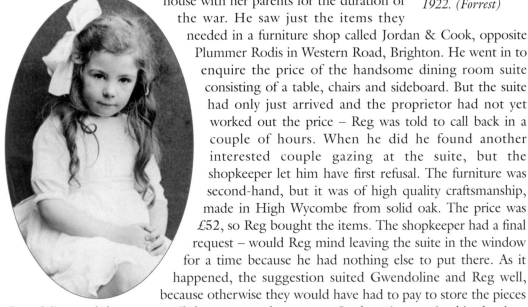

Reg at St Andrew's School, Portslade, in 1922. (Forrest)

Reg had an amusing story about wartime shortages. After being demobbed he and Gwendoline were thinking of moving to a place of their own after having shared a house with her parents for the duration of the war. He saw just the items they needed in a furniture shop called Jordan & Cook, opposite Plummer Rodis in Western Road, Brighton. He went in to enquire the price of the handsome dining room suite consisting of a table, chairs and sideboard. But the suite had only just arrived and the proprietor had not yet worked out the price – Reg was told to call back in a couple of hours. When he did he found another interested couple gazing at the suite, but the shopkeeper let him have first refusal. The furniture was second-hand, but it was of high quality craftsmanship, made in High Wycombe from solid oak. The price was £52, so Reg bought the items. The shopkeeper had a final request – would Reg mind leaving the suite in the window for a time because he had nothing else to put there. As it happened, the suggestion suited Gwendoline and Reg well, because otherwise they would have had to pay to store the pieces until they were ready to move. So the suite remained in the shop for about four weeks with a large notice on the table 'Sold to Mr Forrest of Portslade'. Many of his friends saw it and remarked, 'Nice bit of furniture there, Reg.' The suite became Gwendoline's pride and joy and she looked after it carefully. It was still doing duty in the Forrest home in the 1990s.

Gwendoline aged three, 1919. Her father, Frank Peters, was maint-enance foreman at Portslade Gas Works and goalkeeper for the Gas Works Football team. (Forrest)

Reg married Gwendoline on 4 April 1942. The bridegroom is in his RAF uniform and the bride and bridesmaid are wearing dresses of dusty pink. The bridesmaid is Joan Peters, the bride's sister. (Forrest)

Below: *The wedding breakfast took place at 14 Abinger Road. The man in profile in the left foreground is Tom Puttock from the Mile Oak Waterworks, a cousin of the family. (Forrest)*

14

Betty Figg

Life in an Old Cottage

The Petersfield Laundry in Old Shoreham Road, Portslade, might not seem like a romantic location, but that was where John Tidy and Daisy Blaber fell in love. It was a miracle that John Tidy had a job at the laundry at all; although he had returned home safely from service in the Royal Horse Artillery during the First World War, he came back totally deaf, the noise of exploding shells having shattered his eardrums. His mother assumed he would be unable to do an ordinary job again and had purchased him a smallholding at Mile Oak. Although he was grateful – and he kept the smallholding – he was determined to get back to his old job of maintenance engineer. And he did.

He relied on lip-reading, but his wife learned sign language so that she could communicate with him when he could not make out what people were saying. People had to face him and say their words clearly if he was to lip-read. But of course they did not always bother. What made him furious was when other people directed questions about him to his wife as for example, 'Does he take sugar?' The one advantage to his affliction was when the couple quarrelled. It did not matter if his wife shouted at him at the top of her voice, he would simply turn his head to one side and shut his eyes.

The young couple lived with his mother, Mrs Jenner – John Tidy was born from her first marriage. The family home was at 50 High Street, one of the old flint cottages. Gran was a figure of some authority in the family but she doted on her granddaughter, named Elizabeth after her, who was born in 1925. The cottage was far too cramped for a home birth, and so Elizabeth (everybody called her Betty) was born in a maternity home in Portland Road, Hove). Later on, the Tidys had a son.

Young Betty was close to her Gran, which was just as well, seeing as they shared a double bed. The bed was a huge iron and brass affair with brass knobs at the corners. There was a lovely feather mattress and the bed was covered with a snow-white coverlet crocheted by Gran. The bedroom was too small for a cupboard, and so their clothes were stored in boxes under the bed. Betty had one set of clothes for the summer and another for the winter – the set not in use being put far away under the bed. There was, however, a small chest of drawers over which hung a picture of a blackamoor. Gran said it was a fine painting, but Daisy and Betty both hated it

Petersfield Laundry, 1907. The new works shown here were opened in 1896. (Brighton & Hove Libraries)

because the face had menacing eyes that followed them around the room. Betty often begged her Gran to remove the picture or at least turn its face to the wall, but Gran always refused. Years later, after Gran's funeral, one of the first jobs they tackled was to take down the hated picture and burn it. On another bedroom wall was a huge landscape of Jerusalem, which was not threatening at all, but nobody can recollect what became of it.

On Gran's side of the bed was a commode for her exclusive use, which Betty was never allowed to use – not even in an emergency. There was a marble-topped washstand with a traditional jug and basin, and a tumbler of water for Gran's teeth. It was assumed that Gran performed her ablutions in the bedroom, since she was never known to set foot in the family bathtub. There was of course no heating in the bedroom, so when Jack Frost was about Betty was given a brick warmed in the oven and wrapped in piece of blanket to take to bed with her. There were only two bedrooms upstairs and Betty's parents and brother shared the other bedroom. Gran had the luxury of gaslight in her bedroom, but the occupants of the other one had to make do with candles.

There were two rooms downstairs – the scullery and the kitchen/living room into which you stepped down from High Street. The floor was composed of red bricks set into the earth. There was a basket fire on the hearth and later on a kitchen range, which had to be black-leaded frequently. There was gas lighting, but gas mantles were delicate affairs and tricky to clean; they broke easily and it cost 4½d to buy two new ones.

Space was so limited that the only place to put the copper was under the stairs. No doubt the fire brigade would have been appalled, but the fire was lit under the copper on a Monday morning and the clothes set to boil. An implement called a copper stick (actually made of wood) was used to lift the steaming washing out of the copper to be rinsed in cold water in the sink. The washing was then mangled outside the back door and hung out to dry. If Monday happened to be wet, the washing was festooned over lines in the scullery. When engaged in the weekly wash, Daisy wrapped a piece of sacking around her waist to keep her clothes dry. She had a number of aprons with a strict use for each. There was a starched, white apron for cooking, a wrap-around affair for housework, a coloured pinny for afternoon wear and a posh apron to wear for opening the front door. A knock on the door was always followed by a flurry of apron changing, as no self-respecting housewife would dream of answering it clad in sacking.

The fire was also lit under the copper on a Saturday night when the family took their weekly bath. The tin bath was taken down from its hook on the wall outside the back door and brought into the scullery, where it was filled with hot water – a jug-full at a time – from the copper. Betty's brother, as the youngest child, had first use of the bath water, then it was Betty's turn, followed by her mother and finally her father. It was a cosy way to have a bath in the warmth of the scullery. The only drawback was if somebody opened the back door when there would be a blast of cold air. The choice of soap was not exotic – it was either Lifebuoy or carbolic and it had to serve as shampoo as well.

There was a well in the garden which had provided water for four cottages in the old days, but by 1926 the cottages had piped water with a cold-water tap in each kitchen. However, the cottages still shared an outside privy block at the end of their gardens, close to the wall of the newspaper shop in South Street. There were partitions, but it was possible to hold conversations with your neighbour or your neighbour-but-one while you were about your morning business. (In the adjacent cottages lived the Williams at no. 48, the Patchings at no. 46 and the Darbys at no. 44 – Mr Darby was on the buses.) For a child, the worst time to pay a visit was when it was dark. There was no lighting and so it was a case of creeping down the garden path carrying a hurricane lamp that cast flickering shadows. Once inside you had to light the candle kept there for the purpose. When it was dark Daisy and Betty often went in a twosome; then one could keep watch outside while the other was inside. It was a necessary precaution, because men staggering out of the Stag or George would often make use of the privies if caught short. It was one of Betty's chores to cut up squares of newspaper and thread them on a length of string for use in the privy.

Daisy Blaber and Jack Tidy in the 1920s in a photograph by H. W. Tubb. (Figg)

The old flint cottage at 50 High Street. (Author)

Gran made appetising soups and kept a good stockpot to which she constantly added ingredients – the stockpot was boiled up daily. Suet pudding was on the menu every day, either as a savoury pudding or served with treacle for afters. Chicken was a rare treat reserved for Christmas Day. Christmas decorations were simple; just a few sprigs of holly placed behind every picture (with red beads added if berries were sparse) and loops of paper chains stuck together with a flour and water paste. The children hung up stockings in anticipation of a visit from Father Christmas and he left each one an apple, an orange, a sugar mouse, some chocolate coins wrapped in gold foil and a few nuts.

Gran came from Uckfield but claimed French descent – perhaps her ancestors were of Huguenot stock. Maybe her French genes had something to do with it, because she made beautiful wine in large stone crocks. She used berries and flowers which grew locally and liked to experiment with different varieties. She also made potent moonshine. She had an old friend who worked at the Brewery opposite and he slipped her some malt now and again.

Gran was an excellent needlewoman too and made clothes for the family as well as producing lovely crochet work. But one homemade dress had unhappy memories for Betty. Gran purchased a roll of material from Blackey, the tallyman from Leicester Villas, and created a colourful set of curtains. Unfortunately for Betty, there was enough left over to make her a dress. How she hated it. The material had a black background and was covered with large, brightly coloured fruit such as apples, pears, plums, oranges and cherries. Betty was obliged to wear this creation to school where she was teased unmercifully. She used to come back covered in pinch marks where her tormentors had pretended to pluck fruit. It was pointless to complain to Gran because there was far too much good wear left in the dress to discard it.

During the Second World War Daisy ran a café in High Street near the family home and where the model shop used to be. Here she catered for Canadian soldiers quartered in the village, to whom she became something of a mother figure and listened to all their troubles. If a young soldier got too drunk at the pub for his own good, she would allow him to sleep it off upstairs while keeping his pay-book in a safe place. Next morning she returned the pay-book to the young man with a warning not to be so silly again. When it was time for the soldiers to move on she waved them goodbye, wiping her eyes with a corner of her handkerchief, and saying how much she would miss her boys. But she soon made friends with the new intake.

For years after the war her mantelpiece would be crowded in December with Christmas cards sent from Canada.

Next to Robin's Row stood the old farmhouse with a dew pond nearby. In front of the farmhouse was a sunken lawn on which croquet was played. A gypsy family lived in the farmhouse for many years. When Portslade Grange was demolished and its grounds developed for housing in the 1930s, Betty stood and cried while Gran watched with her arms crossed muttering darkly, 'No good will come of this, you mark my words. They're tearing the heart out of the village.'

The Village Stores in High Street was a traditional sort of shop where you could buy practically anything and Gran did not have to go far for her shopping. It also served as the post office.

The old bridge that gracefully spanned the west end of High Street was demolished in 1946 to allow double-decker buses to travel up the hill. At the same time tall trees along Mile Oak Road were cut back for the sake of the buses. Before the bridge came down, the bus service was a single-decker no. 9 that terminated at the Waterworks.

During the war Betty served in the ATS, getting married in 1945. In 1948 she went to live on a strip of land once owned by Mr Jupp and called Hell Fire Corner. This land was near to where Stonery Road meets Mile Oak Road. Jack Tidy helped Betty's husband move their worldly goods up the hill. They hired a handcart from Mr Kent, the greengrocer, for 10*s* and one man pushed while the other pulled. The move was done at night so neighbours would not see the bed and baby's cot piled up on the cart, but as it was dark a hurricane lamp had to be hung on either side of it.

Hell Fire Corner was full of lovely trees. Betty was very upset many years later when they were felled to make way for Stonery Road. Betty thought she could hear the fourteen elm trees screaming as men hacked at the roots and bashed away at the trunks. They left behind one solitary elm, which succumbed to Dutch elm disease in the 1980s. All along Mile Oak Road there used to be little wooden huts, complete with rain barrels, iron stoves and stack pipes that stuck up like exclamation marks. Gran told Betty that the occupants were establishing squatter's rights.

To the west of where Stonery Road is now there were piggeries belonging to Mr Mason, while to the east were fruit trees. The steps leading down to Valley Road mark Mr Huggett's right of way to his market garden. Where Downland Court stands today was once the home farm for the Industrial School; Mr Lindup was the farm bailiff and Mr Rook was the

Mrs Patching outside the back door of 46 High Street in the 1930s. Her husband was a chimney sweep. (Figg)

A class at St Nicolas's School, 1930. Betty Tidy stands at the back. (Figg)

cowman. The former Spar shop premises in Mile Oak Road was once a large house called Hayracks and another old name is the Vera Cruz Cottages, which are also in Mile Oak Road but opposite Chalky Road. There was a sausage factory in Mile Oak, which was constructed by German PoWs during the First World War. Later on Mr Melville used it as a warehouse to store his theatrical props.

In the old days everything was delivered by horse, from the milkman to the Co-op delivery man, and from the drain cleaner to Dr Brown. Dr Brown cut a remarkable figure in his long, black, cavalry cloak, which was capacious enough to keep his horse's hind-quarters warm; while on his head he sported a black, wide-brimmed hat similar to those worn by French clergymen. Many was the time Betty watched him hitch his horse to a ring at the foot of the drive and walk up to the Industrial School. But Charlie Ayers arrived by bicycle – he was the lamplighter and it was his job to light the gas lamps at evening and turn them off in the morning. Charlie embarked on his working life in 1913 when he was still a boy. He chopped up firewood and the clergy would help him deliver it to the old folk.

15

The Fords

A Family Saga

The coincidence behind the printing of this piece is a story in itself. As a result of the booklet *Memories of Old Portslade* (1991), two women who were once pupils together at St Nicolas's School, Portslade, in the 1920s, met up again after an interval of sixty-two years. It so happened that Mrs Ward's daughter purchased her a copy of *Memories* for Christmas, but could not resist showing it to her mother beforehand. Mrs Ward recognised Gladys Banfield (née Ellis), but had no idea of how to get in touch with her. Then some relatives came up from the West Country to celebrate Mrs Ward's sister Edith's ninetieth birthday. While they were in Sussex, they decided to visit St Nicolas's Church (where they had been married) one Sunday morning. Who should come up to them to have a friendly word at coffee afterwards but Gladys Banfield. When Kathleen Ward (née Ford) and Gladys finally met, they talked for hours. There was another coincidence too – they discovered they were married on the same day – 31 July 1937.

But to return to the story of the Ford family. Alfred and Lucy Ford lived at Cowper Street, Hove, where their first child, Edith Annie, was born in 1900. Some unknown benefactor left a basket of beautiful baby clothes on the doorstep to welcome the new arrival. The Fords never did discover the identity of the donor, but Mrs Ford was so pleased with the gift that she took her baby to Mr Wright, the photographer, at 26 George Street, Hove. The result is a charming study pasted on to stiff card, and it is obvious that the clothes left plenty of room for growth.

There were to be six children of the marriage. The next child, Harry, was considered rather delicate and the doctor advised them to move to the country where they would enjoy purer air. They moved to Portslade! However, the move must have been beneficial to young Harry because he grew up to be fit enough to join the Royal Navy and became a chief petty officer.

In 1903 the Fords moved to a house in Wolseley Road, and the following year Ethel was born; Sid followed in 1907. An eccentric resident of Wolseley Road was Madame Manetta who looked after the goats that pulled little goat-carts full of children along Hove seafront in the summer. During the winter the goats moved into the house with her. Naturally, the children were wont to tease Madame Manetta who retaliated by threatening to fetch the police. On one occasion when one of the

St Nicolas's Girls' School Bazaar and Sale of Work, 4 June 1913. Edith is in the back row, third from right. The teachers are Mrs Sayers and her daughter Miss Sayers. (Marriot)

Ford boys was ill in bed with scarlet fever, he happened to glance through the window and saw a policeman striding along the bridle path at the back of the houses. He was terrified and shouted to his mother, 'Don't let him take me, Mum.' Nursing a case of scarlet fever at home was somewhat demanding. A sheet soaked in disinfectant was hung across the bedroom doorway and Mrs Ford kept a separate set of clothes to wear inside the sickroom.

Another serious illness in the Ford household was Harry's Spanish Flu. It was not a mild sort of flu but a virulent kind, which swept through Europe like the plague after the First World War. The death toll was enormous. In Harry's case he became ill away from home and his mother hired a cab to bring him home to his own bed. The cab halted at the level crossing gates and Harry promptly fainted. Mrs Ford clambered down and knocked on the door of the railway cottages (where the public loos are today) for assistance and a glass of water. Eventually, they reached home safely, but Mrs Ford strained her back in her efforts to half-carry Harry upstairs.

The fifth child, Kathleen, was born in 1914, after which the Fords began to find the house in Wolseley Road a little cramped. In 1916 they moved to a more spacious house in Norway Street and Mrs Ford was more than happy with it. They would have stayed indefinitely, but the engineering firm CVA (forerunner of Kearny & Trecker) purchased the houses for their workers and the Fords had to move on. This time it was to a house in Victoria Road, and their landlord was a Mr Bungard whose relatives ran an undertaking business. Mr Bungard was a kindly man and whenever he heard of sickness in the family he always turned up on the doorstep with a jug of hot broth.

The children often played in the sand and flint pits where Vale Park is today. One day Sid, aged ten, and Kathleen, aged three, were playing with another little girl there. Then Kathleen was taken home while the other two continued to play. Suddenly the sides of the sand pit collapsed on top of them and they were buried. People came running to help but the little girl was found dead. Her parents were in the audience at the Hippodrome and had to be informed of the tragedy. As for Sid, although completely buried, he managed to dig his way out. However, afterwards he had a lifelong fear of sand and cliffs.

The children went to St Nicolas's School. Edith remembered the sewing class where the girls made surgeons' gowns for use at Hove Hospital. Sewing was considered a useful accomplishment, and indeed, it became Edith's favourite occupation. She was never without a piece of sewing or crochet work. It was the cause of a spot of bother later on when she went to work at Ronuk. In high spirits one day she swung her bag around and the ever-present crochet hook managed to embed itself in another girl's arm. The matron insisted that she kept a cork on her crochet hook from then on. But Edith's sewing skills were invaluable to the family, because she was able to copy any item of clothing that they might fancy. Sewing also came in useful for providing items for the St Nicolas Sale of Work.

Another event in the 1920s school calendar was dressing up for a tableau or a dancing display. Mrs Sayers was particularly keen on dressing up. Sometimes it was not immediately obvious from the costumes just what the girls were meant to be, but the parents understood it was Mrs Sayers's version of whatever it was – little Dutch girls for instance. Of course the costumes had to be devised from whatever was to hand, as there was no extra money to splash about. Kathleen remembered taking the part of Sleeping Beauty and her costume consisted of Mrs Sayers's best petticoat!

Unfortunately, Sleeping Beauty could not pretend to be in a deep sleep because she was overcome by a fit of giggles, and the splendid petticoat quivered throughout the tableau.

Miss Watson, owner of Portslade House, used to donate a Christmas tree

The Ford family, November 1907. Left to right: Ethel, Harry, Edith and Sid with Kathleen in front. Mr Ford wears the uniform of the Royal Engineers and next to him is his wife Lucy. (Marriot)

to the school every year, together with presents for the pupils and some parents. One year Mrs Ford was excited to receive a present and opened it with eager anticipation. But she was very disappointed to find it contained a delicate fan. 'What use is that to me with five hungry kids?' she remarked somewhat ungraciously.

Alfred Ford always tried to find a job. If he was out of work, he tramped the streets for hours looking for work of any kind. An enduring memory of his was of his first-born Edith crying with hunger when there was nothing in the house to give her. As a child Kathleen remembered gazing through the window at Bungard's café in Victoria Road to watch workmen lifting the crusty lids of their large pork pies to pour in brown sauce. How she longed for a pork pie of her own. But when she grew up and began to earn her own living, she found that the attractions of consuming a pork pie had long since faded.

Mr Ford was a strict father, but this did not prevent his children from getting into all sorts of mischief. Their rule was that if they had been naughty they would rush upstairs to bed to escape a good thrashing. They knew their father never entered the bedrooms.

The house in Victoria Road was near the railway yard where cattle and pigs were kept overnight after being off-loaded from the goods train. They were destined for the slaughterhouse off Wellington Road. The animals sensed what was to happen and set up a tremendous bellowing and squealing. To prevent young Kathleen from being upset, she was told the noise came from the Gas Works and was nothing to worry about. For years she firmly believed that the Gas Works was responsible for those curious sounds.

There used to be a piece of wasteland where Hallyburton Road is today and gypsy families used to camp there to earn money at harvest time. The local children were rather afraid of them. Sometimes gypsies banged on the door to demand water, but the Ford children were too scared to answer. A favourite gypsy ploy was to ask a shopkeeper to change a 10s note at the same time as buying an item – they hoped to confuse the shopkeeper into forgetting to charge them. But people soon became wise to this ruse. There was one occasion in Clark's Bakery when the gypsy was so angry at his trick failing that he chased the assistant round and round the shop. It was fortunate that a male customer appeared in the nick of time.

Most of the Ford's cooking was done on an unreliable range, which was not trusted when an important birthday was imminent. When Harry was away in the Navy over his birthday, it was the custom to despatch a homemade cake to him. Mrs Ford would mix all the ingredients together, place them in a tin and ask one of her brood to take it to the baker's shop in Abinger Road to be baked in its oven. Once it was Kathleen's turn to run this errand. On the way to Abinger Road she stopped because her arms ached and rested the tin on a convenient hedge. Unhappily, the tin tipped over and the precious mixture oozed out on to the ground. Kathleen burst into tears and a kind passer-by helped her to scoop it all up again, throwing out the odd piece of chalk in the process. The cake was duly baked and sent off to Harry who pronounced it to be the best cake ever.

Lucy Ford's maiden name was Chappell and her brother Sidney Chappell joined the 1st Battalion Royal Sussex Regiment in 1905. He saw service in Malta, Crete,

Belfast and in India. His regiment was still in India when he came home on leave in 1914, bringing a fine shawl and a parrot he had taught to speak but not to swear, so as not to upset his female relatives. Had he stayed with his regiment in India, he would no doubt have survived the war. As it was, he was sent to France where he was killed on 14 September 1914 at Vendresse, less than two months into the war. His name is on the memorial in Easthill Park. Before embarkation for France he had proposed marriage to an Irish girl. She sent him a letter turning him down, but it is not known if he heard the news before he died.

Edith remembered hanging out of the window of the Ronuk factory with the other girls to wave goodbye to soldiers as they marched along the road on their way to the Front. However, Mrs Ford did not think Ronuk was good enough for her daughter, and when she saw an advertisement for a cashier at a greengrocer's shop on the corner of Lansdowne Place, Hove, she made up her mind this

Sidney Chappell of the Royal Sussex Regiment was killed on 14 September 1914. (Marriot)

was the job for Edith. She marched into the manager's office at Ronuk and announced her daughter was leaving at once. On being informed that a week's notice ought to be given or a week's wages would be lost, she replied loftily, 'Then we'll leave the money.' On Edith's day off mother and daughter went out on a 'two girls together jaunt'. Edith was under strict instructions not to call her 'Mum' and Lucy was furious when she forgot.

In 1920 the Ford's sixth and last child was born – a daughter called Doris. It was a great tragedy when Mrs Ford died six weeks later at the age of forty-one. The event changed Edith's life completely. She had to leave her job and lose her independence. Instead, she took on the role of housekeeper and looked after her siblings. There was the baby as well as six-year-old Kathleen and thirteen-year-old Sid. Edith was only nineteen and had to learn how to run a household through trial and error. The range was a particular bugbear, and it was difficult to ensure food was properly cooked – there was one dinner Sid called Edith's half-cooked stew. When Edith shopped at places where the family was not known, people noticed the baby and no wedding ring on her finger, and treated her with contempt, thinking she was an unmarried mother. There were lighter moments too. One day when Edith was busy in the kitchen a horse suddenly put his head in through the door. She was not to know that her mother had befriended the horse that pulled the coalman's cart and the horse had called for his customary lump of sugar. Unfortunately, later on the accumulated strain and hard work of running the house and looking after the family made Edith ill for almost two years.

Kathleen Ford married William Ward on 31 July 1937. Kathleen's sisters are bridesmaids – Doris is on the left and Edith is on the right. (Marriot)

In 1935 her father, Alfred Ford, remarried. His new wife was a widow with four children of her own, and so she did not have much time for her husband's children from his first marriage. Kathleen remained at home until Doris left school when she was fourteen. Doris became a live-in mother's help and Kathleen went to live with her aunt in Hastings Road, Brighton. The move to her aunt's house changed Kathleen's life, because she promptly fell in love with her first cousin, William Ward. At first the family had grave reservations about the relationship because of possible medical implications, but after a chat with the family doctor they relented and gave their blessing. William and Kathleen married on 31 July 1937, and of course Edith made the bride's and bridesmaids' dresses. Kathleen was evidently in no hurry to hear the patter of tiny feet. In fact, it was thirteen years before she gave birth to their only child, a daughter. Her doctor was taken by surprise as he thought she had indigestion!

16

Charlie Todd

Serving in Dad's Army

Although Charlie Todd was born in Watford in 1912, he reckoned he was a Portslade man because his family moved there when he was three years old and he has stayed ever since. His various addresses in Portslade include Wolseley Road, Abinger Road, an old flint cottage near the Southern Cross pub (demolished in 1974) and Melrose Avenue. The family moved to Portslade to get away from wartime air raids in London in 1915. Charlie's father, Mr Todd, senior, was a watchmaker and jeweller by trade, and although he returned from war service all in one piece, he had been gassed and was never the same again. He died in March 1925, and the British Legion took up the case to ensure Mrs Todd received a war widow's pension of 10s a week. She needed every penny she could lay hands on, as she had five children to care for, and the youngest, Muriel, was only a year old. For six terrible weeks, no money came into the household at all. But the neighbours did what they could to help out. Charlie particularly remembered one man who sent him home with a tray of jam rolls.

The boys earned pocket money where they could. A favourite method was collecting horse manure, of which there was a copious supply just waiting for them on the roads. They could sell a barrow-full to keen gardeners for 6d, and it only cost 1¼d to get into the picture palace. On 24 April 1924 Charlie and Jack Todd saw a grisly street accident, but the boys took it in their stride and stood staring at the corpse until a teacher from their school ushered them away. The unfortunate man was George Street, a famous Sussex cricketer, who crashed his motorbike into the wall near Tate's Garage.

The Todd children attended St Nicolas's School, and Mrs Atherfold made a lasting impression on Charlie. He remembered her way of instilling good manners into infants of five. She would take her seat in the doorway of the hut where the infants were taught and the morning ritual went like this.

'Good morning Miss Atherfold.'

'Good morning Charlie.'

'Please may I pass by you?'

'Of course you may.'

Miss Atherfold would rise and allow the child into the classroom before resuming her seat and awaiting the next child. When Charlie went up to St Nicolas's Boys'

A wonderful photograph of an outing to the Northampton Shoe Factory, c. 1932. It was arranged by the Co-operative Women's Guild (Portslade Branch). Mrs Todd is seated second from the left in the front row. (Todd)

School, it was Mr Burn who next impressed him. Charlie remembered him as a giant of man, and truth to tell, the boys were somewhat scared of him and his Northern wit. Many years later Charlie discovered Mr Burn was still alive and living locally, and so he went to visit him. He was amazed to find that the redoubtable figure was quite a small man after all. Mr Burn lived to the ripe old age of ninety-six and his unmarried daughter looked after him.

For a man who was to earn his living as a carpenter, Charlie Todd did not have a very auspicious start. During a carpentry lesson Charlie was busy working on a piece of wood with a jack plane when along came a boy called Len who pinched it. Well, Charlie saw red, snatched back the plane and gave Len a thump on the head for his presumption. Unfortunately, the blow knocked Len out and Charlie was sent home in disgrace.

When war broke out in 1939 Charlie volunteered for the Armed Forces. But he was never called up because his skills as a carpenter were too valuable. He was kept hard at work in the Lady Bee Yard at Shoreham Harbour as a carpenter in the engine room of a variety of vessels in need of repair. He worked on torpedo boats, MGBs, MIBs, and MLs, to name but a few. Once he went aboard a French vessel where the captain knew all about the British sailor's supposed fondness for rum or 'neaters', as it was known. He offered Charlie a tot, but Charlie certainly never bargained for the almost full tumbler he was handed. He thought he would explode as he downed it in a few gulps, and has never been able to look rum in the face since. That afternoon he had arranged to meet his wife in Shoreham where he was supposed to offer her moral support, because she was due to have some teeth extracted at the dentist. But all he could do was sit in his chair and giggle.

On 15 June 1940 Charlie joined the Home Guard. His unit was E Company F Platoon 14th (Hove) Sussex Home Guard. It really did bear some resemblance to television's successful comedy show *Dad's Army*. There was an elderly volunteer called Private Allen who was sixty-three years old, and Jock Cameron, Company Sergeant Major of B Company, was mad keen on bayonet drill. There was Dixie Dean, an ex-Army man, who was meticulous about the shine on his boots and was never seen without his war medals. He had a florid complexion.

But at least the men drilled with proper rifles and not ash staves, as happened in some rural units. Granted, they were not the most up-to-date models, indeed they were rifles from time of the Boer War and measured some 6ft 6in with a 16in bayonet, but they weighed about the same as a standard Enfield.

On one occasion Charlie was on duty at the foot of Station Road in the blackout. He heard footsteps coming towards him and called out the customary challenge three times. There was no reply and the footsteps kept on coming forward and so Charlie decided it was time his rifle saw some action. He pulled the trigger – and nothing

The Home Guard outside Ronuk Hall, c. 1943. Back row, left to right: Bob Partner, Dixie Dean, Len Souter, Arthur Harris and Len Searle. Middle row: Ted Perry, Matt Coomber, Lieutenant Smith, Lieutenant Richards, Sergeant Todd and Corporal Charlie Clarke. Front row: Sid Hibbard, Stan Gibbs and Bill Maynard.

This cartoon was published in Night Hawk, *the magazine issued by the 14th Battalion (Hove) Sussex Home Guard, in February 1941. (Author)*

happened – the rifle had jammed. It was just as well as it turned out, because the footsteps belonged to an Irish labourer who was a little the worse for wear.

The Home Guard's HQ was in the old Brewery building in Portslade Village, on top of which an anti-aircraft gun was mounted. The Home Guard companies took it in turns to mount guard at the various posts in Portslade. The guard posts were as follows:

1. East Tower of the LCC School (the old Industrial School) Mile Oak Road
2. Waterworks, Mile Oak
3. Dyke Hovel (about halfway between New Barn Farm and the Dyke)
4. Gas Works and beaches
5. Portslade station
6. Foot of Station Road

Charlie recalled two amusing incidents that occurred when he was on guard duty at Dyke Hovel. It was in 1940, just after the evacuation of Dunkirk, and everyone was a little jittery, expecting the Germans to invade at any minute. One night those on guard duty were convinced the balloon had gone up, because they could clearly hear Jerry soldiers marching along the road with a steady tramp. A cautious reconnaissance revealed the true culprits – a herd of cows happily pulling up grass and munching. Then there was the time the blackout was pierced with hundreds of tiny shining lights. It seemed quite possible that the lights were attached to German paratroops and the men felt that the Downs were probably alive with Jerries. This scare had a natural explanation – it was a colony of glow-worms. There are still glow-worms there to this day, although unhappily much reduced in numbers.

The occasion when a real German landed on the Downs was a time to remember. It happened that a German ME 110 was shot down over Shoreham, but the pilot managed a skilful landing at Erringham. He was perhaps luckier than he realised, because he managed to avoid trip wires placed about 100yds apart that festooned the area. Charlie saw the incident and jumped into a two-seater Morris to race up to the turnip field where the aircraft had landed. Right next to it stood a green-faced German pilot with his hands in the air. Just as Charlie half believed what Lord Haw-Haw said about the atrocities German soldiers would commit when they got here, so the trembling pilot must have heard horror stories about British soldiers and wondered what his fate would be. But it was all handled in a gentlemanly fashion.

Training was a serious matter – there was plenty of rifle practice and route marches, sometimes wearing respirators. The training ground was on Slonk Hill. The 49th Edmonton Regiment from Canada and the Welch Regiment, neither of which had yet received much formal training, were often observers of Hove Home Guard's training programme. Some of the training was quite hair-raising, as live ammunition was used. It was certainly one way of ensuring the men learnt to keep their heads down. There were bound to be accidents. One of Charlie's colleagues dropped a live grenade near him and the resulting blast deafened him in one ear for life.

Another exercise involved C Company having to travel at night from Shoreham to the Gas Works without being detected by Southwick Home Guard. Apparently the most hazardous part was crossing the railway line in the blackout. C Company had almost made it and was coming along North Street near the Windmill pub when Southwick Home Guard spotted them. A thunder-flash was launched, which dropped almost spent at Charlie's feet. His automatic action was to kick it away. He was not to know that the pub's cellar doors were wide open and down the thunder-flash went, causing a great deal of noise and confusion. The top brass made a pretence of a court martial for such unseemly conduct, but all Charlie really received was a slap on the wrist.

In 1944 Charlie volunteered for secret work. On 3 January 1944 he was told to proceed to Portsmouth Harbour and he would be given directions from there – so to and from Portsmouth he used to go evening and morning. He had no idea what it was about and he was not best pleased when he realised it was night work. Neither was his wife. They had recently moved house and she had a 10-month-old daughter to look after. As Charlie needed to sleep during the day, Mrs Todd spent a fair amount of time wheeling the baby about the streets in its pram so that Charlie would not be disturbed. The hours were long too, as he was gone from 6.30 p.m. to 8 a.m. He continued to work on this project for all of 1944 and some of 1945. The secrecy was because he was working on the famous Mulberry Harbour project, which was to play such an important part in the Normandy landings. He helped to construct the shuttering into which reinforced steel was placed and concrete poured. Each section was 118ft long, 30ft wide and 60ft high. The great day came when a section of the works was flooded to see if the Mulberry Harbour was effective. There were plenty of scoffers who expected the project to fail, but instead it was a success.

17

Doug Mepham

A Portslade Gassie

The Mephams were all 'Gassies' – that is they were employed at the Gas Works. There was George Henry Mepham and his brother Bert, and George Henry's son Doug, and they all worked at Portslade Gas Works. George Henry's other two sons followed the family tradition elsewhere; Jack went to Watford Gas Works and Archie worked at the Hove Yard where the gasometers were situated next to St Andrew's Old Church.

G.H. Mepham was Foreman Engineer at Portslade Gas Works, and he and his wife lived in Franklin Road in about 1900. There were six children in the family and besides the boys already named, there were three girls – Elsie, Dorothy and Marjorie.

The family's next home was in Beach Bungalows, which were situated on the beach, west of where the Seaside Villas of Western Esplanade are today. It was a wonderful place in which to bring up children with the sea right on the doorstep. However, it was not quite so rosy in winter when strong winds sent waves crashing over the cottages. But at least the air was clean and fresh, which was more than could be said of the vicinity of Wellington Road where windowsills were always caked in coal dust and even the grass in the small back gardens was sooty.

Beach Bungalows were technically within the Parish of Aldrington, and so when Doug decided to get married, the banns had to be called at St Leonard's Church. His bride was Winnie Drew, whom he had met at Portslade St Andrew's Youth Club. There is a splendid photograph of a church outing from St Andrew's, which took place on 22 July 1922; the happy couple are sitting in the vast charabanc and in close attendance is Winnie's mother, Mrs Drew, looking somewhat grim-faced. The Drews lived in Wellington Road, and perhaps the continual battle against the all-enveloping coal dust had worn her down. Sometimes there

Doug Mepham in his Boy Scout uniform, c. *1915. (Hayward)*

Doug Mepham as a young man.
(Hayward)

were compensations for living there, such as the occasions when all the ships in the canal would be decorated to celebrate some important event.

Winnie earned her living as a domestic servant and she was two years older than her husband. They married on Boxing Day 1925 at St Andrew's Church, Portslade. Mr Mepham snr was unimpressed by the romance of a wedding, and as his son only earned 25*s* a week, he told him he would have been better off buying a new pair of boots instead!

Doug Mepham must hold some kind of record, because he was a Portslade 'Gassie' for fifty-one years. He started work there at the age of fourteen and stayed on until his retirement in 1968. Being a Gassie was more than a mere job – it was a way of life with social activities thrown in. The men took pride in the works and the machinery was always gleaming – there was a great deal of rivalry between Portslade and other Gas Works. Doug's Uncle Bert was Chief Officer of Portslade Gas Works Fire Brigade and they were rather good at winning competitions – Doug often carried away a first prize certificate.

St Andrew's Youth Club, c. 1918. Mr Bear who ran the Portslade branch is standing on the left wearing a straw boater. Mrs Drew sits in the second row from the front, third from left. Her daughter Winnie sits next to her. (Hayward)

An outing from St Andrew's Church, 22 July 1922. Winnie Drew is seated in the centre wearing a large, dark hat. Doug Mepham sits next to her and Mrs Mary Drew stands behind her daughter. (Hayward)

The Drew family, c. 1906. Left to right: Fred, Philip, Mary, Winifred and Frederick. The boys were twins. (Hayward)

Portslade Gas Works Fire Brigade in the 1920s. Doug Mepham stands in the back row, second from right. (Hayward)

Doug was also interested in first aid and joined the Southwick Division of the St John Ambulance Brigade. He and another man were founder members of the Portslade Divison, of which he became Superintendent in 1946. In 1960 he was a made a Serving Brother of the Order in honour of his many years of service. But he made no mention of the honour when he went off to London to receive it. Many other certificates were found among his papers after his death.

Knowledge of first aid came in useful at the Gas Works, and Doug was often the first one on the scene after an accident. On one occasion his family teased him about losing a pair of trousers at work; it was only later that they learned that he was obliged to act quickly to prevent an explosion and fire – his trousers were saturated with oil. At other times he enjoyed regaling his family with sundry gory details when they were trying to eat their dinner!

The Mepham family, Winnie, Doug and two daughters, lived in Wellington Road. Gwen was born in 1927 and Joan in 1937. The family moved to Fishersgate in 1937. Joan remembered the Fishersgate house as always being full of people. Doug ran the Unity Youth Club in Fishersgate Hall and people often popped back for a cup of tea. There were also musical evenings when the family had a singsong around the piano and Doug performed on his brass penny whistle, musical saw or violin.

Doug enjoyed amateur dramatics as well, and took part when the Gas Works put on plays. Some of the workers were so good at playing the accordion that they formed themselves into the Gasco Band, playing at local hops and dance halls. Why the drum bearing the legend 'Gasco' was decorated with a lady in a crinoline is something of a mystery.

As a young man Doug used to put in a full day's work at the Gas Works before going to evening classes at Brighton Technical College. He continued doing this for five long years until he had passed all his exams and become an AME. But his hard work paid off because he became Mechanical Superintendent at Portslade Gas Works. His old headmaster, John Miles, wrote a testimonial for him 'to all it may concern' dated 6 November 1937:

Mr Douglas Mepham has been known to me from his infancy and during seven years was a scholar under my care at St Andrew's School, Portslade-by-Sea, where he passed through the various classes with perfect credit to himself. Since leaving he has vigorously pursued his education by attending Technical Schools etc. and has sought progress in every way open to him. Of his personal character I cannot speak too highly.

Portslade Gas Works Fire Brigade, 1937. Bert Mepham is behind the wheel and Doug Mepham stands on the far left. (Hayward)

Canadian Joe Taylor from New Brunswick was stationed at Portslade during the Second World War and used to spend his leave with the Mephams. His two brothers who also served in the armed forces were killed. Joe was a PoW for two years, but managed to survive despite being ill and emaciated. When he recovered and got married he sent this photograph of the happy occasion back to his friends in Portslade. (Hayward)

One ambition he did not realise was to serve in the Royal Navy during the Second World War. He regularly applied to join but was always turned down, because he was in a reserved occupation and could not be spared. But he did what he could to aid the war effort and invented a modification to the stirrup pump by which an incendiary bomb could be extinguished without the operator having to go inside the room into which it had fallen. He was an Air Raid Warden as well, and when the siren sounded out he went, closely followed by his daughter Gwen, who could not bear the thought of being trapped inside during an air raid. All in all, it must be said that Doug led a very full life indeed. In recounting it to me, even his daughter Joan was surprised at the amount he managed to pack in. He died in 1977.

18

Ernest Charles Moore

Life at the Gas Works

It was a good thing that Mary Ann Virgo was used to being part of a large family, because when she married Percy Edward Moore in the 1890s she soon began to produce her own numerous brood. They were Daisy, Bill, Fred, Ernest, Gladys, twins Annie and Ethel, Violet and Bert. Somehow the family managed to fit into 2 East Street, Portslade. There were three bedrooms, but even so the children had to sleep three to a bed. In the winter the boys took it in turn to sleep in the middle of the bed squashed between the other two, because this was the cosiest place. Families of this size were not uncommon in those days, and there was a camaraderie because most of the men worked at either the Gas Works or the brickfields at Wish Meadow (Wish Park), Aldrington.

The privy was in the back garden and there were hutches full of rabbits and a few hens scratching about. It all helped to supplement their diet and provide some eggs, but roast chicken was a treat reserved for Christmas. Mrs Moore's home fire was kept burning with the help of her industrious children, who were always on the lookout for small pieces of coal that sometimes fell off passing wagons. Cooking was done over the fire, but her bread oven was not large enough to take a joint. Luckily, she knew Mr Mason the baker, and when there was a joint to be cooked, it was taken to his bake-house and placed in his huge oven.

Mr Moore worked at the Gas Works, and in the days before there was a canteen, his wife or one of the older children used to take his dinner to him over the canal in the small ferry. The food was put on a plate and tied up in a red-spotted handkerchief, known as a Tommy handkerchief, because Tommy was the nickname for food.

Ernest Charles Moore was born in 1901 and left St Andrew's School, Portslade, at the age of thirteen. In November 1915 he started work at Portslade Gas Works and earned 10s for a 12-hour day. He was only a lad, but he was given an enormous shovel, the handle of which came up to his chest, and told to start turning over the bog ore (oxide). It had to be given a good airing and it was a regular chore. It was the mounds of greeny-red oxide which were responsible for the Portslade Pong – that is the smell of the Gas Works that permeated the clothes and skin of the men working there. The old workers grew impervious to it and so presumably did their wives. But the reek would practically knock an outsider for six. The Portslade Pong spread over

The huge expanse of Portslade Gas Works on the south bank of the canal in the 1920s. Although Portslade was densely packed with housing, there were still undeveloped stretches of Hove. (Masters)

the canal into the houses of much of South Portslade, where it lay like a pall when the weather was still and cloudy. Indeed, sometimes it was so powerful that residents suspected a major gas leak and would send for the local gasman to come and investigate. This was still happening right up until the 1960s. Another legacy of the Gas Works was the thick mantle of coal dust that spread everywhere.

Town gas was more noxious than North Sea gas. Sometimes, the fumes would overcome a worker, and he was brought outside and laid in the open air. When he revived he was given milk to drink, as this was considered the best antidote to absorb poison quickly. Then he was walked about until he felt better and could return to work. Being knocked out by gas was no excuse for going home early, and besides he would lose his wages. It is probable that prolonged exposure to gas affected the personality of some workers over the years. There was one man who turned increasingly violent as time passed. Any excuse or none would set him off into a rage. Another man who was overcome by fumes and staggering about in the open air was so deranged he began to punch a horse that happened to be standing there.

Horses were used to pull tip-carts, and the Gas Works owned two powerful shire horses as well to pull the barrow containing the pump maintenance equipment. Local men such as Mr Field, Mr Trigwell and Mr Penfold who ran small businesses all had tip-carts, which were regularly seen at the Gas Works. The horses were stabled at East Street or George Street – both in Portslade – and they soon became familiar with Gas Works routine. When the steam hooter went off at 5.30 p.m. in the summer and half an hour earlier in the winter, the horses knew it was knocking-off time and would start off for their stables on their own initiative. Of course, they could not use the quick way across the canal by ferry like the workers, but had to go the long way round by Hove Lagoon.

The steam hooter went off regularly at other times of the day, for instance at 6 a.m., 8 a.m. and 1 p.m. People would set their watches by it, and it was a useful check for those households that did not boast a clock. After the First World War on Armistice Day, the hooter sounded at 11 a.m. and everyone who could downed tools to observe the two-minute silence.

The colliers carrying coal to the Gas Works were quite small vessels (around 800 tons) in the old days because the canal was shallow and could not accommodate anything larger. As it was, the pilots were kept busy easing vessels in and out of the canal. Two of the men Moore remembered were Pilot Grant and Pilot Upperton. On the subject of names, some of the earlier colliers were called after the directors of the Gas Works, hence *John Miles* and *FE Webb*. There was also a *Portslade* and later colliers were *JB Paddon*, *Hove* and *Steyning*. A charming name belonged to the barge that plied up and down to the Britannia Flour Mills during a strike – her name was *Rosebud*.

It was astonishing how rapidly the coal could be removed from the boat when there was little else to rely on except muscle and experience. It was claimed that 100 tons could be off-loaded in an hour. If a man did not pull his weight and was deemed not to be working hard enough, his mates would sing out, 'Wagons up, my hearties!' The routine was to have eight men down in one hold and eight down in the other, with one man on lookout at each. There was one crane driver to each hold and he let down a tub weighing half a ton to be filled with coal. When full, it was hoisted up to the stage by the tram road and two tippers transferred the coal to the carts. Then the wagoners (sixteen of them altogether) pushed the carts along the tram road, some to the North Retort, others to the South Retort. On arrival a special catch on the wagons was knocked up and coal poured out on to a grating. The men who shovelled the coal down through the grating were called knockers-down.

Another old-time task was called head-stoking. It sounds quite alarming but what it meant was stoking the coal into the furnace by a deft thrust of the shoulders. Men filled a scoop with coal known as a fiddle-stick, hoisted it to their shoulders and approached the furnace at a run; a quick flick over of the fiddle-stick and the coal shot into the furnace. This method meant the men spent the minimum time in close contact with the fierce heat. Later on of course, these jobs were mechanised. The coal was tipped into the retort by means of a hydraulic wheel, which the workers

The horses working for the Gas Works were well looked after. This is Bobby, one of the old stalwarts, in 1888. (Brighton & Hove Libraries)

The interior of part of the Gas Works in the 1930s. (Hayward)

nicknamed the Iron Man. Likewise, the unloading of colliers was made a great deal easier by the introduction of what was called the donkey crane.

A standard joke at the Gas Works was that it turned out old men and coke. However, during the First World War so many men were called away to the Armed Forces that the management was obliged to employ around 150 women and boys, plus a few pensioners. The women expected no favours and proved to be hard workers, even though much of the work was tough and physical. There was talk of employing PoWs but the workers strongly opposed such a move. In the event PoWs did not arrive at the Gas Works until 1919, being marched down daily under armed guard from Brooker Hall (now Hove Museum). There was uproar, as people believed that the Germans would sabotage everything in sight, so the management had to issue a reassurance that PoWs would not be allowed anywhere near the gas-making plant; they were to be confined to shovelling clinker and other tasks in the outside yards.

When Ernest Moore started work at the Gas Works Mr Rutter was the manager. He lived in Beach House right by the canal (the house was later demolished). Succeeding managers were Mr Smallbone and Mr Corfield. There were other changes over the years; for example the round retort was changed to a 'D' retort, and a 36in gas main replaced the old 24in size. The company also expanded, taking over the Worthing Gas Company in the 1930s.

The ferry linking the Gas Works to the north bank of the canal has already been mentioned. What is perhaps not generally known is that these boats were built in the carpenters' shop at the Works. They were unusual little vessels, because they were double-bowed – that is pointed at each end. This was found to be the most stable model for a small boat crossing a stretch of water often beset by south-westerly gales. None ever capsized, and in the interests of safety there were always four oars aboard. There were about seven or eight of these boats, nicknamed cockle-shells, tied up by the dock wall. A boat could hold sixteen men at a pinch or a single workman could row over by himself.

A rather different sort of boat was the magnificent three-masted schooner *Ludwig Reediman*, which went aground on the beach behind the Gas Works. A storm blew her on to the beach in about 1915, but eventually she was floated off. The beach was reached from the Works by a wicket gate, and the pebbles were useful as ballast for ships that had just unloaded.

The layout of the Works was something along the following lines. At the east end there was the carpenters' shop and paint shop. Then came the administrative part and offices. Next was the old blacksmiths' shop, and opposite was a large piece of waste ground, which, after the First World War, was made into a sports field where football and cricket were played – there was a bowling green as well. No. 1 Engine House was next to the field; by the middle road stood No. 1 Retort, No. 2 Retort and No. 3 Retort, then came the water plant, followed by a screen nicknamed Dolly Gray where the ashes and waste were sieved out. After that came the new blacksmiths' and fitters' shops.

Moore left the Gas Works in 1940. It was not exactly voluntary as he was called up into the Army. The Gas Works tried hard to keep hold of their workers, but Moore's work was not classified as skilled, so he could not claim to be in a reserved occupation. So off he went. But as he was the grand old age of thirty-nine he was not despatched to the Front. He joined the 6th Royal Sussex Regiment and spent the duration guarding German PoWs, first at Beaconsfield and later in Hanover. After the war he did not return to the Gas Works but took advantage of the co-partnership scheme, whereby he was entitled to draw a lump sum. Then he went to work in the foundry run by Briggs & Baker next door to the old Rothbury Hall.

Brighton & Hove Gas Company's twelfth Annual Sports, 1 September 1923.
(Brighton & Hove Libraries)

19

Frederick Charles Hill

of Hill's Radio

Frederick Charles Hill was born on 19 October 1910 in Church Road, Portslade. His maternal grandmother's family were hatters from Luton and his mother arrived in Sussex to work as a nanny to a wealthy family who lived in a large house in Ashdown Forest. She enjoyed her work and was well cared for, but it was customary in those days to resign one's post on marriage. Her husband was Tom Hill who worked on a local farm. Then came a time of hardship in the countryside, so the Hills were obliged to move to try and find work, which is how they came to Portslade.

Tom Hill took employment at the Britannia Flour Mills run by Sundius Smith and his brother. The Smiths were an important local family: one brother lived in an impressive house called Zion Lodge in Station Road and the other in Courtney Terrace, a little higher up the road. Tom was originally taken on to look after the four horses used at the Mills, but then he became involved in all aspects of milling, ending up as foreman. The Britannia Flour Mills were situated at the south end of Church Road and had a private wharf fronting the canal where the ships and barges used to unload. There were two old flint-built cottages nearby in Church Road called Mill Cottages, and in one of them lived the Hill family.

Fred Hill had a wonderful childhood, which might have had something to do with being the youngest child – he had four much older siblings, William and Arthur, Winifred and Elizabeth. So there were plenty of people to make a fuss of him. He was a particular favourite of his father, who in later years would take him fishing or to watch cricket at the Sussex County Cricket Ground. Fred Hill's first memory is of a sweet shop in North Street and the serious tones of the grown-ups as they discussed the implications of the outbreak of the First World War. Around the same time the Hills moved to 19 Church Road, Portslade.

The war disrupted the pattern of work and many women were employed as labourers at the Gas Works after the men had left to fight. Fred can remember these women, trudging up Church Road, after finishing work, clad in bulky overalls with their skin an unhealthy shade of yellow, caused by sulphur fumes. Although Fred was allowed to attend the cinema in North Street on Saturday mornings, his mother forbade him to go up the street in the evening. This was because there were five pubs in the area and a great deal of drunken behaviour.

St Philip's Church was consecrated in 1898. This view was taken before its enlargement in 1909 to 1910. (Author)

First Fred went to the Infants' School in St Peter's Road, followed by some years at St Andrew's School, Portslade. Many of the schoolchildren came from poverty-stricken families and arrived at school in worn clothing, while some had no shoes on their feet. One master at the school was John Miles (no relation of the 'aircraft' Miles family) who was also choirmaster at St Andrew's Church, Portslade, where young Fred became a star choirboy and sang many solos. The choirboys were paid half a crown a quarter, but if they were naughty, a penny was docked from their earnings. One day Frederick took part in a Christy Minstrel show and afterwards he was approached by the choirmaster of St Philip's Church, Hove, who offered to pay Fred double the money he was earning. When Mr Miles heard about this, he was furious, and he stormed round to the Hills' home to complain. But Mrs Hill said it was up to Fred to decide what he wanted to do. He chose to go to St Philip's, but he missed the old church, his friends and scrumping for apples in Hillman's apple orchard just over the wall from the church. He stayed at St Philip's until his voice broke, then he left choir work for good.

Fred's best friend was Tom, whose father was landlord of the Crown and when Fred was twelve or thirteen he used to help out at the pub. In doing so he met all sorts of interesting characters, including captains of windjammers still sailing into Shoreham Harbour. For some it was a regular run and he got to know them well; one offered to take him on a trip to London to load up the ship and then return, but his mother would not allow it. Other regulars came to the Crown for a lunchtime sandwich and a beer, including Frederick Miles and Cecil Pashley, who were hard at work constructing an aircraft in the yard of the Star Model Laundry in

Wellington Road. The Miles brothers later became very famous in the aircraft industry, while Pashley was a noted early pilot. Fred and Tom often went back with them to the laundry to watch progress or over to Shoreham Airport to help out. If anybody booked a 5s joyride, the boys helped to haul the plane out of the barn and then Pashley took them up. When it was time to signal to the plane that it should return they used a novel device. This was a large tin sign advertising Reckett's Blue (for laundry) and they simply turned it around so that the silver back reflected the sun. At other times the boys helped to entertain the waiting queue. One trick involved four balloons placed on a sandbag barrier. Pashley came out and with a flourish produced a pistol (filled with blanks) and shot three balloons, but missed the fourth to the groans of the crowd. Meanwhile, Fred was hidden behind the sandbags and it was his job when he heard the bang to prick the balloon – the fourth was left unharmed on purpose. The *pièce de résistance* was when the crowd saw Fred's arm rise above the fourth balloon and deliberately pop it – then they realised what had been going on. Needless to say, when they boys wanted a joyride themselves they did not have to pay.

Fred and Tom often used to play along the banks of the canal, and they were well acquainted with the entrance to the underground tunnel, which legend has it was linked to smuggling operations of old. They never ventured inside – besides the entrance had become very overgrown, and if the occupant of the nearby Crab House spotted them he would chase them away. The tunnel was supposed to lead to the Downs. The Crown had deep cellars and there was also believed to be a smuggling tunnel leading from the inn to St Nicolas's Church. Stories were told about the smuggling days, and one old chap told Fred that the smugglers used trained dogs to swim from the smugglers' boat to the shore at Copperas Gap attached to small barrels. The work was not too hard for the dogs because, of course, the barrels floated and they were nothing like the size of an ordinary cask – they were miniature, about 2ft in height.

A summer diversion was grass bank sledging. Fred used to haul his curiously carved sledge all the way to Cockroost Hill, and then he would enjoy a long slide down. When he and his friends were thirsty they called at the Waterworks and asked to fill their bottles with water. Fred remembers the lovely bee orchids that grew on Cockroost Hill.

Fred left school at fourteen and joined his brother Arthur at the Home & Colonial Stores. His other brother William was a butcher in Southwick, while both his sisters worked as nannies until they married. But Fred hated the job and he could only stick it for five months. Then he became an apprentice joiner at John Eede Butt, the timber merchant. This was more to his taste and the apprenticeship lasted for three years. Then in about 1928 Arthur and Fred Hill decided to start their own business, which became Hill's Radio, and was situated at 42 Boundary Road, next door to the Co-op.

There they stayed until late 1939 when they were called up promptly, because of their radio skills – the Government took three of four radio specialists from the locality including the man from Lambert & Whistlecroft near Palmeira Square.

The Hills were sent to Cranwell for their training and they were horrified at the antiquated radio equipment they found there. Arthur joined the Army and went to Bletchley Park, while Fred went to Gatwick where 116 Squadron was being reformed. At Gatwick there were Spitfires, Tiger Moths, Ansons and Oxfords. Fred was sent all over the place, including France and Scotland, and when the war ended he was in Norway. (By the way, he likes to remind people that his moustache pre-dates his RAF days). Back in England, he was demobbed with a blue pin-striped suit with turn-ups and a waistcoat to match, a pair of civilian shoes and a gratuity of £100. Meanwhile, Arthur had decided to stay on in the Army; the old shop had been let, so Fred took another shop at 25 Boundary Road. But he always wanted to move further up the road because he reckoned there was more trade. His next stop was at 35 Boundary Road in the early 1950s, and by 1956 he was at 36 Boundary Road. There he stayed until he moved across the road to 41 Station Road, Portslade, where he set up shop in about 1963.

Fred Hill with his wife Helen and son Michael walking along Western Road, Brighton, c. 1950. (Hill)

The business is still in existence – greatly expanded and with the new name of Hills Sound and Vision.

Fred encountered a number of characters over the years in his shops. For instance, there was Old Man Peters, who was a market gardener. On one memorable occasion in the 1950s he came into the shop in his grimy gardening gear, pointed to a handsome Marconi radiogram and growled, 'I'll have that and I want it tonight'. Whereupon he put his hand in his pocket and peeled off £25 from a wad of notes – a considerable sum in those days. Another customer who expected instant service was Mrs Broomfield from North House Farm, who, when her TV went wrong, expected someone to call on her the next minute. An early 9-in black and white TV was purchased by Sister Joseph of the Little Sisters of the Poor who took it back to the Old Folks' Home her Order ran in the Old Shoreham Road, Hove (the site now covered by Homebase). Whenever there was a storm, Fred came to expect a call from Captain Nell of Western Esplanade – his TV aerial was always being broken by the wind. But he must have loved living there because his living quarters were designed as a cabin, complete with portholes and a binnacle.

Fred Hill married Helen, a Brighton girl, in 1942. They made their home at Treetops, a house in Mile Oak Road with a garden full of trees. There were three large elm trees bordering the footpath leading to Drove Road, but these and other elms in the garden (a total of thirteen) had to be felled later because of Dutch elm disease. They had an Alsatian dog called Trigger, who was very popular in the neighbourhood and good with children. However, he was not so fond of dustmen, and once gave chase to the Portslade binmen (one tall, the other short) who dropped their bins and jostled each other to get out of the gate first. One Sunday morning at 7 a.m. Trigger was found sitting menacingly at the foot of a ladder up which a hapless couple from Mile Oak Gardens were trying to rescue their cat – Trigger had chased it up a tall tree. The Hills had two children – Michael (who became a civil engineer) and Andrew (who manages Hills Sound and Vision). The Hills stayed at Treetops until the 1970s.

20

Eric Masters

Buses, Lorries and a Portslade Childhood

It was a family tragedy that made George Masters move from London to Brighton. He was born in 1895 and had two older sisters called Alicia and Ethel and a younger brother called Leonard. Their father followed a skilled trade – that of a compositor in Fleet Street. Typesetting consisted of fitting tiny lead letters and figures in lines to make up a page of print. It was fiddly work and Mr Masters was continually licking his finger in order to get a better grip on the pieces of type. He was only thirty-one years old when he died of lead poisoning. The family believed that lead also affected the youngest child Leonard, who died at the age of thirteen.

Mrs Masters found herself unable to cope with four children. The girls were old enough to be useful about the house, but poor George was sent off to Stockwell Orphanage where he spent several painful years. His pathetic letters to his mother are still treasured by the family. In about 1910, when he was old enough to leave the orphanage, he decided to make a fresh start with an aunt who was living at Brighton. The institution sent him off with the gift of a Bible that had 'Stockwell Orphanage' stamped in gold on the front cover, and the headmaster's signature inside. By this time his brother was dead and his sisters were married and working as waitresses at Lyons' Corner House in Holborn.

During the First World War Masters spent three years with the Army Service Corps, Sussex Yeomanry. The experience gave him a useful passport to civilian life, because it was the Army that taught him to drive motor vehicles. He was invalided out with rheumatic fever, and when he had recovered he took a job with Southdown driving one of their motor buses. His career on the buses proved to be more far reaching than he expected, because it was there that he met a pretty young clippie by the name of Marie Mitchell. Marie's family lived at 15 St Nicholas Road, Portslade. So many men were away fighting in the war that employers were obliged to take on young women for what had been regarded previously as men's work. Even so, the company would only take young women aged eighteen or over, and so Marie had to stretch the truth a bit because she was only sixteen when she applied for the position. She must have been proud of her job and the smart uniform, because she

Marie Mitchell wearing the uniform of a Southdown bus conductress with modifications on her part because her skirt was shorter than standard issue, c. 1917. (Masters)

lost no time in going along to Mr Tubbs, the well-known Portslade photographer, to have her portrait taken. The result was fetching, and it is interesting to note how fashionable her boots would be today. However, her skirt was a different matter. Apparently, Marie decided that the length of the regulation skirt, which came just above the ankle, was too long and so she shortened it herself. The authorities were far from amused and she was almost dismissed because of it. (Marie was born in Adur Terrace, Southwick, right next door to the birthplace of the celebrated contralto Dame Clara Butt.)

George and Marie were married in 1921 and went to live with her parents in St Nicholas Road. Marie's father was employed in constructing the intriguing Mystery Towers at Shoreham Harbour. The war ended before they could be put to use, and for a while local people were allowed, on payment of 6*d*, to row across the canal and climb to the top for a superb view. One of the visitors was Marie Masters who sturdily staggered to the top, even though she was seven months pregnant with Eric. However, at the top realisation set in – she simply could not get down again under her own steam. Whether it was the height or the difficulty of seeing the steps with her bump in the way, we shall never know. But she had to be carried down. When one of the Mystery Towers was towed out on a high tide Mr Mitchell went with it. It was a tight squeeze and Mitchell always maintained the tower got out to sea with only a leeway of some 18ins on either side. He stayed with the tower until the Nab was reached, where he worked on filling it up with concrete – it became the base of the Nab Lighthouse. Then he was employed at Portsmouth and Mrs Mitchell went to join him, leaving the young couple in the house at St Nicholas Road.

As soon as Marie's labour pains began she sent for Nurse Holder, a Queen's Nurse who lived in St Andrew's Road. In fact Nurse Holder attended all three of Marie's births – first there was Eric, then Gordon and finally June. June went on to become a Lecturer at Northbrook College of Technology, Worthing, and lived in a house some 300 yards from the old family home where she was born.

One of Eric's earliest memories is of his mother taking him to Fishersgate Terrace to wave to his father who was driving Southdown bus no. 31 from Brighton to

Portsmouth. (In the 1920s the usual working day was 10 to 11 hours long.) The journey took some 4½ hours, so Marie took along some sandwiches and a flask of tea. The bus had solid rubber tyres and was a double-decker with an open staircase at the back leading up to the top deck, which was open to the elements. There was no glass windscreen for the driver's cab in those days; in foul weather the only protection a driver had was a tarpaulin sheet that came up to chin level.

The General Strike of 1926 did not affect Southdown very much, although Tilling's and the Brighton buses did not leave the depot. Southdown was tough with drivers who did strike – they were sacked. After the strike Southdown said it would never employ a man belonging to a trade union. Although George Masters did not strike he became fed up with the poisonous atmosphere and decided to set up his own business. He purchased an old AEC lorry (BP 5669) and set up his transport business. He would take on anything – bricks, timber, sand, clinker – and slowly he built up his trade.

Meanwhile, the Masters children were going to school, starting off at St Peter's Infants' School, where Miss Turner was the headmistress, and then to St Andrew's School, Portslade. Miss Bunting was headmistress at St Andrew's and Eric was amused to learn that she had also taught his mother. Miss Bunting lived three doors up from the fire station in Church Road and the brass door-knocker was in the shape of a Lincoln imp. Eric also remembered Miss Kaye and Miss Diamond at the same school. Miss Kaye was of ample girth. She lived in Brighton and could not manage to get there and back for her midday meal, so she came to a splendid arrangement with a lady living in Brambledean Road. Every school day her friend cooked her dinner and carried it to the school. The dinner was on a covered plate and on top a smaller covered plate containing pudding, the whole ensemble secured with a chequered cloth. There were no school dinners in those days, so all the children went home – the dinner break lasting for nearly two hours.

Sir Alexander Gibb designed the Mystery Towers as a sophisticated submarine barrier – although of course the general public did not know that at the time. (Jeeves)

Many of the children came from poor families and around 30 per cent did not have any socks to wear to school. Among the boys, favourite pastimes were collecting cigarette cards and playing marbles. The common or garden marbles were made of earthenware, but the more valuable ones were glass alleys with their different colours and spirals. Another popular object on which to spend pocket money was a do-it-yourself photographic kit available for a few coppers at a shop on the corner of Albion Street and North Street. The kit consisted of a small piece of frosted glass, a frame and a sheet of sensitised paper. You put it all together and stood it at an angle in the sun for ten or fifteen minutes while the photograph slowly developed. The photographs were of buses, cars, ships, animals and various scenes.

When Matthew's Fairs visited Portslade, which they did two or three times a year, Eric and his friends were sure to be in attendance. It is interesting to note the different sites where the amusements were set up. One site was south-west of Church Road, north of the canal, where the old Texaco terminal used to be; another site was south of the Crown, near Britannia Wharf. When these sites were no longer available, Matthew's moved to the south-east corner of what is now Vale Park, where the Tandy Laundry used to be. In those days it was rough ground, some of it used for sand and gravel pits, and there was a steep cliff (or so it seemed to the children) by Hillman's quarry. Vale Road was not then a through road, and so people used the ground as a short cut to get to Portslade station – it went past the Catholic church and past Hillman's cliff and on to Station Road. The youngsters also went to Sanger's Circus

Nurse Holder (right) was something of a Portslade institution – loved and feared in equal measure. She organised this Bonny Baby Contest. (Author)

when it came to Hove in the 1930s. The big top was erected in a field north of New Church Road, diagonally opposite Wish House near Aldrington Recreation Ground.

The main shopping area in Portslade was still North Street and there were at least four butchers' shops there. In the 1930s some of the butchers were Charlie Mathewman, Charlie Hamblin and Fletchers. On Saturday night at 8.30 p.m. there was always a crowd of people, because that is when the butchers used to auction off their meat cheaply – it was better then letting it go to waste. On the corner of Church Road and North Street was the Police House, then came a hairdresser's, a fish shop and finally the Picturedrome cinema. The cinema and the two small shops were knocked down in about 1930 and the new Pavilion cinema built on the site. During the building work exposed electricity cables were left sticking out of the ground and the local lads used to make them flash sparks – it was amazing nobody was electrocuted.

Next door to the Masters's home lived Mr Brooker, the local representative of the Brighton & Hove Gas Company. Every day his wife polished, with the help of a tin of Bluebell metal polish, the brass plaque on the door carrying this information. Mr Brooker was on call at all times to assist customers. He went everywhere on his bicycle with a pump and suction hose strapped on his back. It often happened that when someone's gas pipe was blocked, a quick blast from his pump would do the trick.

Eric's last school was East Hove Senior Boys' School in Connaught Road. Here there were classes of forty-nine boys so strict discipline was essential. By this time Eric was famous for being a chatterbox, and one headmaster recorded on his report

Two Morris commercials belonging to Masters & Smelt, c. 1927. (Masters)

that he 'overworked his tongue'! But his hands were also busy, and in 1934 he was awarded a certificate of merit at the local Models Exhibition when he made a single valve radio set.

During the Second World War Eric spent five years in the RAF as an aircraft engine fitter, which gave him a great deal of valuable experience. After leaving the RAF Eric took a job with Brighton & Hove Bus Company, but he did not stay there long. After three months he had a disagreement with the management over what he regarded as unfit buses and malpractices, so he left. Years later he was amused to discover the company had endorsed his record with the note 'this man must never be re-employed'. In 1947 Eric took over the haulage business from his father – he was the only one who could do so, because his brother Gordon went down with HMS *Hood* when he was just a boy sailor aged sixteen. George Masters then went on to run the Jolly Sailors, a pub in Wellington Road. In those days that part of Portslade was still heavily populated with pubs – there were the Crown and Jolly Sailors in Wellington Road, the Clarence, the Clarendon and the Windmill in North Street, the Cricketers in Church Road and the Halfway House, Blue Anchor and Railway Tavern in Station Road.

Meanwhile, Eric continued to expand his haulage business, until, by the mid-1960s, he had a fleet of sixteen lorries. George Masters and Marie died within two months of each other in 1979, and in 1980 Eric decided it was time to retire. But after six months, he became bored and for the next eight years he was engineer and assistant manager of Volk's Railway. Eric and his sister June are still residents of Portslade.

21

Pam Dry

A Friend at Easthill House

Pam's maiden name was Dugay and she came from a family of railway specialists working for the London, Brighton and South Coast Railway. Her grandfather, Samuel Dugay, was one of the instigators in the electrification of the line (although he left school at thirteen and was self-taught) while her father Ernest Charles Dugay (known as Sonny) was Chief Linesman. Pam's first job was with Southern Railway, in the ticket refund office at Redhill. The unusual family surname originated in France, the Dugays having come to England from the Channel Islands. Sonny was transferred to the Brighton area in 1934, which is how the family came to live at Fairway Crescent, Portslade, in 1936. Pam, an only child, was aged seven at the time. From her bedroom window she could see the train travelling slowly towards Devil's Dyke.

The house backed on to a market garden – now covered by Dean Gardens – where fruit and vegetables were picked. In fact, the surroundings were still quite rural, although some development had started. Mill Lane was just an unmade track and there were only two semi-detached houses to the south of it. Mr Goacher, who lived in Old Shoreham Road, cultivated two large fields. One was known as Goacher's Buttercup Field and was near the top of Mill Lane – Pam used to walk past it every weekday on her way to St Nicolas's School. (An unexploded bomb landed on this field in September 1940.) The other Goacher's field was between Sharpethorne Crescent and the then top of Benfield Way. It was always known as the Cabbage Field, whether or not there was a crop of cabbages. One year there was a plague of caterpillars and the field turned into an unsavoury, heaving mass, and people stopped using the footpath through it. Near the Mill House was a wooden shed where a couple sold sweets to schoolchildren and refreshments to Comber's workmen. When the parade of shops was built, the couple were the first occupants of the newsagent's shop.

Down the footpath and through the copse, one came to the side entrance of Easthill House, where Pam's best friend June Cleverley lived with her elder sister Madge and their parents. The Cleverleys lived in the older part of the house – the flint two-storey building at the back of the big house overlooking the stable block. Mrs Webb lived in the big house; Mr Cleverley was her chauffeur and Mrs Cleverley

Easthill House. (Author)

her housekeeper. Mrs Webb was a widow of some years standing her husband had been involved with the famous London jewellers Mappin & Webb. Not surprisingly, the furniture and surroundings reflected an elegant taste. Mrs Webb preserved the air of an Edwardian lady with her ramrod straight back, hair piled on top of her head, long skirts and long-sleeved blouses into the 1930s. However, the girls did not see much of her, as they played at the back of the house, but the few glimpses left a lasting impression.

The stables were by then disused and Pam and June found them the perfect place in which to play houses. They put up curtains, arranged their furniture and had tea parties. When they felt more energetic they went in for acrobatics on the horizontal poles laid across the side entrance. They also enjoyed helping the gardener. The kitchen garden was north-east of the house, and on one occasion June inadvertently plunged a garden fork through her Wellington boot and her foot, which caused a great commotion. Presumably their garden visits were curtailed after that.

During the Second World War Pam moved up from St Nicolas's School to Hove County Grammar School for Girls. As part of the war effort the girls took part in fruit picking during the summer. One season they were sent to Peacehaven to work among the sugar beet, while another season they stayed at Horsted Keynes where they picked plums, blackcurrants, greengages and early apples. If the weather was bad they did a stint in Hartley's Jam Factory instead. It was hot, dusty work and they slept in tents with the local church hall as their community area. They were young and it was a novel experience, so they found it fun despite the sinister Doodlebugs overhead.

After one such expedition, when she was sixteen years old, she was walking home to Fairway Crescent, hot, tired and somewhat dishevelled when she happened to meet a young man who had rented a garage there. His name was Leonard Dry and he was hard at work on his motorbike, which he was mad about – he also had a Morgan three-wheeler. Leonard had studied electrical engineering at technical college in Hackney, so the authorities sent him to do war work at CVA, the local engineering firm, which constructed machinery to make parts for planes and guns – he had lodgings in Mill Lane. They hit it off immediately and he often used to meet her at school on his motorbike – to the envy of the other girls, no doubt. Pam left school when she was sixteen and she and Leonard married in August 1949. They took their BSA three-wheeler on honeymoon to Cornwall. Their two boys continued the family interest in motorbikes and one of them took to racing them at well-known venues. The Drys were married for fifty-two years until Leonard died.

22

Desmond Leonard Stevens

From Post Office Messenger Boy to REME

Desmond was born on 24 May 1925 in St Aubyns Road, Portslade, the last in a brood of seven children. His elder siblings were Ethel Marina (the eldest) Percival Lionel, Horace Frederick, Cecil James, Donald Henry and Robert James. By Portslade standards the Stevenses were relatively well to do because Mr Stevens earned £3 10s a week, and their house was the first in the street to have electric lights installed. Mrs Sharp came in to help with the washing and cleaning. In 1939 Mrs Stevens purchased a Beatty washing machine, which was quite a novelty. Mr Stevens was a master dyer and was Works Superintendent at Flynn's, the well-known cleaners and dyers.

Des went to St Peter's School, Portslade, and remembered his first day as a somewhat tearful occasion. He watched the iron gates close and his mother walk away. He had to stay there for the entire day, although subsequently he went home to lunch. Two older boys noticed his tears and called him a cry-baby and there were comments about the shine on his shoes. When it was lunchtime he found a bench at the back of the school and sat down to eat his food. But the bullies followed and sat down too. Then he bent down and somehow managed to tip the boys off the bench – he was never bothered again. Other boys who had been bullied came up to speak to him. Discipline was harsh and one incident stands out in his memory. One morning at assembly the headmistress came in with a boy who had tied a little girl to a tree, leaving her there when he went home. The headmistress said severely, 'We do not tolerate such behaviour.' She then applied the cane to the back of his legs and he was a very sorry sight at the end of it. The rest of the children were horrified, but it taught the boys a lesson that however rough they were with each other, they must not attack little girls.

Des's next school was St Andrew's School, Portslade. It is interesting to note that Esperanto was taught there, although it never carried on beyond two terms. He enjoyed learning the new language and thought it should have been taught universally – he can still remember bits today. He was not allowed to come home from school by the direct route, because his mother thought the junction at the foot of Church Road and Wellington Road was too busy and dangerous – the Britannia Flour Mills being situated near at hand. Even so the area had a fascination for the boys, because there was a blacksmith's shop opposite the mill. When the blacksmith was in a good mood he would let the boys stand against the wall and watch the dray horses being shod.

A favourite play area was the land now occupied by Vale Park. In those days it was sand pits and as the sand was removed two hills, as it seemed to the children, remained. They were called Cabbage Hill and Butterfly Hill and gangs of exuberant boys would constantly fight over their ownership. The gangs were local boys, but if the Goodings gang, who came from outside Portslade, turned up the game would hot up considerably. When the dishevelled Stevens boys arrived home the worse for wear, they would receive a good hiding or else be grounded. Another game played on fine evenings was 'he' or 'tag', when the boys would hide and wait to be discovered. Once Des and his friend ventured into Baker's yard where coffins were constructed. They heard approaching footsteps and squeezed into one of the coffins. The light was switched on and the men came to collect the coffin they were hidden in. Although the friends were frightened at the thought of being discovered, the two men probably had a greater fright when the lid shot off and the boys hurled themselves out of the yard.

In the summer it was considered quite normal for boys to spend the whole day out on their own, and when the weather was warm Des and his friends made for the beach at the back of the Gas Works. It was an exclusive little spot, because only the locals knew about it. If the boys had a halfpenny on them they took the ferryboat rowed by Mr Hamblin across the canal – it cost one penny return. At that time the new lock gates had not been installed, so when the tide was out the boys had to wade out to the ferryboat or be carried. If they did not have any money it was a long walk around. When they did have some, they would hire a rowing boat and take a trip up the canal. On the way they passed the famous Crab House situated on the north shore. People believed it had connections with the old smuggling days, and indeed there was a tunnel leading from it that went under the road, under Flynn's factory and surfaced at the company's sports centre, known as Champion House. Two of Desmond's older brothers attempted to explore the tunnel but their lighted candles suddenly went out. Mr Stevens was furious when he heard about their adventure. He told them that they would not have been able to come out at the other end because Freddie Flynn had sealed it with concrete. Sometimes the boys visited the Electricity Works to wade barefoot through the cooling ponds situated in that strip of land between the canal and the sea called the 'gut'. They wriggled their toes in the water feeling for any movement and then dug in the mud for dabs, a local delicacy.

At other times the boys headed for the Downs at Mile Oak. They had little carts connected to their bicycles in which to take provisions and tents and camped out on the old firing range. They did not need to carry water as they could always collect some from the Waterworks. In the evening they lit a fire and indulged in a somewhat barbaric sport – catching adders from the field called Adders' Bottom and chucking them on the flames. Other excursions involved walks over the Downs to the Shepherd and Dog at Fulking where there was always a lovely cold drink from the spring to be had or if they were in funds, perhaps a glass of real lemonade. Sometimes they took a trip on the Dyke Railway – it cost 6*d* from Aldrington Halt – and on other occasions they went on a bike ride to Shoreham Airport to watch the planes taking off and landing.

On rainy days they made model planes out of solid pieces of balsa wood they picked up off the beach – you could buy instruction charts for 3*d* or 6*d*. The planes lasted for years. Nearly every boy had an air rifle, and instead of lead pellets they made potato ones to fire at flies on the wall in the garden.

The Stevens paid for their boys to go to Connaught Road School, which had an excellent reputation. Indeed Mr Ralph, the headmaster, wanted his establishment to be recognised as a grammar school, and accordingly taught to that curriculum. But this ambition was never realised, and that and the loss of his son during the Second World War killed him, according to his brother George Ralph. From Des's point of view going to the school had a distinct advantage, because as it was 3 miles distant from his home he needed a proper bicycle. Soon he was the proud possessor of a brand new Hercules three-speed bicycle, a dynamo, a puncture outfit and the proper gear to wear in wet weather such as cape, leggings and sou'wester hat. The weather had to be atrocious before he went to school by bus – the fare costing 1*d*. The school was divided into 'houses' and Des went into Corinthian. He was not worried about his academic work, as he had usually been in the top six at his last school. But he was in for a rude awakening because he had never been taught decimals. Soon he found himself relegated to the 'B' stream, to his intense mortification, but at least he did not have to do book-keeping or typing.

Bob Orme lived next door to the Stevens and went to the same school. When he left he became a boy messenger at Portslade post office. When Des was thirteen and a half, Bob asked him if he would like to be a temporary messenger, working in the evenings, Saturdays and Sunday mornings. His parents agreed and off he went. As the Second World War was looming the postmaster, Charles Smith, asked him to make blackout screens for the post office, which had to be fitted and removed every day. When war was declared the messenger boys were kept very busy delivering call-up papers, and they were allowed to work overtime to keep up with the work. Mr Smith had a word with Des's parents to say he could arrange for him to be released from school early, provided he continued his education with the post office, so he left school at thirteen.

Messenger boys were told to continue with their duties even after sirens sounded and were only to take cover when bombs started to fall. They could go through road-blocks and enter prohibited areas, and naturally felt a sense of importance. This was tempered by the realisation that their arrival was not always welcome because so many men had to leave their wives and families behind. Then there was the horrid task of delivering telegrams with black borders on their yellow envelopes. Most of these went to Bob Orme as senior messenger, but Des remembered one he delivered. It was to the Goble family, whom he knew as they had a greengrocer's shop on the corner of North Street and Station Road; every Friday Mr Goble came round with wet fish displayed on his cart. Des handed the telegram to Mrs Goble who promptly fainted. Mr Goble was at hand, opened the envelope, read the contents and said grimly, 'No reply'. Their son had been killed in action.

A happier occasion was when he delivered a telegram with a gold edge to a man in Old Shoreham Road who had won a substantial amount on the football pools. The man was so delighted that he handed Des a tip of 10s. His mother thought he ought to give it back, but she relented after she had checked it out with the post office.

Meanwhile, the rest of the Stevens family were scattered by the war. Horace was the first to be called up, because he was in the Territorial Army. Cecil became an aircraft fitter and was sent to Southern Rhodesia. Bob was obliged to leave his apprenticeship with Courtney & Burkitt's shipyard and take a post in engineering until he was called up into the Fleet Air Arm – he served aboard HMS *Pioneer*. Percival was in the Channel Islands and Ethel had married Bernard Francis Woolgar and lived in Kent with their two sons. That left Donald at home, and he was not going anywhere because he had been badly injured in a car accident at the age of fourteen and had been in a coma for three weeks. He and Des shared a bedroom, but Des could never settle until after his brother was asleep. This was because Donald had to be strapped into a harness of wood and plaster of Paris to try and straighten his twisted back. The pain was so bad he would cry himself to sleep. One night their mother could stand it no longer, returned to the bedroom and removed the harness, which was never used again.

When Des was fourteen he decided on a change of direction. In order to forge ahead in his career in the post office he would need to take exams, and a good part of them was sending and receiving Morse code, which he was not very good at. However, he had received excellent reports on his woodwork at school, and the upshot of it was that he was taken on as an apprentice at the Jigs, Moulds & Tool Company in Portland Road. He started work on a capstan lathe, shapers, planers, grinders and milling machines. It was a crucial time because so many workers were being called up, so soon a boy was doing a man's job. For instance, Des had to set up three milling machines as deputy to the official setter. Eventually there were no men left in his section, so women operated six machines.

As soon he was old enough Des joined the Home Guard – the 14th Division, Royal Sussex Regiment. His father was in the same outfit but a different section. The 49th Edmonton Regiment (of Canada) helped to train them in unarmed combat, grenade throwing and how to assemble a Vickers machine gun. Live ammunition was used at Mile Oak on the old firing range, while grenade throwing took place at Devil's Dyke. The Home Guard drilled with six Ross rifles but they did not have the ammunition to go with them. Part of the duties carried out by the Home Guard was to guard and protect the Jigs, Moulds & Tool factory and man the telephones in the workshops in case of air raids to report on any damage. As the factory was by the railway line it seemed obvious that it would be a target at some stage.

RNVR call-up at Hove in 1939 – the sailors are from the London Division. The building in the background already belonged to the Admiralty, so they simply requisitioned the new swimming baths next door and the whole establishment became HMS King Alfred. (Brighton & Hove Libraries)

On 24 August 1942 three bombs were dropped on Portslade. One landed on top of Bellman's store in Station Road, bounced up in the air and landed on a house in Worcester Villas where Joan Shepherd held her dancing school. Pupils and teacher survived by diving under the stairs, but Joan's legs were injured by falling wreckage. Another bomb fell on Vine & Lee's premises, also in Station Road, but did not explode. Shrapnel from a cannon shell hit the factory wall in Portland Road and fine debris composed of cast-iron shreds and brick dust filled the air – Des thought at first it was smoke. He and his colleague emerged looking like Kentucky Minstrels, and although his friend's back was bleeding, he returned to work the next day after pieces of brick and metal had been removed from his back.

It was impossible to take a dip in the sea during the war as the beaches were out of bounds, but Des and his friends were still able to swim in the old Medina Baths. They used the smaller one, which was once the Ladies Bath, while the larger one was used as a temporary mortuary. The new swimming baths had been taken over by the

Admiralty to become HMS *King Alfred*. One day Des was cycling along just after noon to take his usual swim and had just reached Hove Bandstand when he heard the deep noise of approaching engines. He looked up and there were three Heinkels looming overhead; he could clearly see the soldier hunched over a machine gun in the forward turret. Bullets sprayed everywhere and Des was knocked off his bike and into the pillar box on the corner of Sackville Gardens. Fortunately he was not hurt, and carried on to have his swim. These hit-and-run raids were quite common during the early part of the war, and usually there were no British planes to see them off.

The crunch for Des came in December 1942. One morning he turned up for work to find that three machines had finished their batch, which meant he would have to spend nine hours fitting them up for new work if he did not receive any help. His foreman promised he would ask Mr George to help once Des had made a start. But Mr George was off sick. This, together with the knowledge that although he did a setter's work he was not an official setter and was paid less because he was not yet eighteen, added to his feelings of frustration. He had tried to join up before, but he was not allowed because he was in a reserved occupation. This time he was determined to be successful, so he got on his bike right away and headed for the recruiting office in Queen's Road. Luckily he found a wonderful Colonel Blimp-type character and not the sergeant he had seen before. The upshot was that he filled in his form, went upstairs for his medical and received the Queen's shilling all on the same day. But the Colonel was obliged to take the shilling back because there was a war on. When Des returned to the factory the management was not amused and said it would get the whole thing quashed. Des had to appear before a Manpower Board in Montpelier Road and relate his story. They upheld his decision to join up. Eventually, he was posted to the Royal Electrical and Mechanical Engineers.

Des Stevens during his first leave, 1943.
(Stevens)

23

Thomas Huntley Wood

The Sailor on Player's Cigarette Packet

Thomas Huntley Wood was born in 1868 at Lyme Regis, Dorset, and entered the Royal Navy at the age of fourteen, serving for a period of twenty-four years and ending up as a Chief Petty Officer. 'His scars, tattoos and countless yarns bore witness to his worldwide adventures.' It was in 1897 that a photographer visiting his ship, HMS *Edinburgh*, in Galway Bay was struck by his fine nautical appearance including a 'full set' (beard and whiskers) and took his photograph. This was later reworked to appear in 1898 as a coloured portrait of Wood framed in a lifebelt carrying the legend 'Player's Navy Cut' with the sea and two ships in the background. Before Wood's portrait was used an artist had drawn an imaginary sailor and put *Hero* on the cap-band, leaving the HMS out in error, not being a naval man. The ship on the left was HMS *Britannia*, a wooden ship with 120 guns.

Wood knew nothing about Player's new design until the picture appeared on cigarette packets. His colleagues must have recognised him instantly and his officers advised him to write to the firm about using his likeness without permission. The clerk who wrote the letter for him suggested that he ask John Player & Son for £15. But Wood thought this was a bit steep and reduced the request to 2 guineas. The letter ran, 'I am quite willing to allow you that permission, providing you give me the nominal sum of 2 guineas and a sample pound of your Navy Cut to allow my mates to test its quality.' The company got a bargain, because by the time Wood died his portrait had been seen by millions of people for more than fifty years. But in the end he became fed up with fame, because everywhere he went some man was bound to pull out a packet of Player's and sing out 'is that you?' In the end there was nothing for it but to become clean-shaven.

When he left the Navy he did not finish with the sea. He became a coastguard and moved to the north of Scotland, where he remained until 1920. He and his wife Rebecca had a large family of seven sons and five daughters, and at least one of them, Emily Florence, was baptised in the Church of the Holy Trinity, Dumferline, Fife. Wood wrote a poem called *The Wreck of the Eutopia, Gibraltar, March 17th 1891*, which began, 'Talking of wrecks at sea sir / It makes my heart feel sore / It reminds me of a wreck I saw / Just off Gibraltar shore.' The *Eutopia* was an emigrant ship from Naples with 1,000 souls on board. She left Naples on 12 March and arrived at Gibraltar five days later, but struck the head of an ironclad just off the new mole head. The battleships fired their guns and Jack Tars rushed to the rescue, but even so 564 men drowned. 'Then our Battleships fired their guns / And every boat was manned / And within ten minutes / They were there to give a hand.'

When Wood retired the family moved to Southwick before buying a house in Ellen Street, Portslade. He was well known there as the man on the Player's cigarette packet. His neighbour, Teddy Emery, believed that he received 10s a year in royalties for the use of his portrait. An interesting letter was published in the *Evening Argus* (22 November 2001) from O.W. Moore whose grandparents owned the Clarence Hotel in North Street. He remembered that Wood often used to sit in the private bar at one of those hard-topped tables with ornamental cast-iron legs and he always wore a naval cap. Sometimes he would perform his special trick for him, being a child of six or seven at the time.

> He would produce a penny from his pocket with his right hand and place his left hand under the table, tap the top of the table with the penny, say some magical words and produce the same penny from under the table is his left hand. I would think two pennies were involved but, at my age, when a child's world was a magical one, to me it was just the one coin with a touch of mystery.

In 1946 Thomas Huntley Wood and his wife Rebecca celebrated their Golden Wedding. He wrote to Player's

Thomas Huntley Wood and his wife
Rebecca with sons George and Charlie
and pets (including the budgie in its cage),
c. 1946. The photograph was taken by
Stacey Wood of 39 Station Road, premises
previously occupied by H.W. Tubb. (Buck)

to remind them of his story and they sent him a gift of tobacco and cigarettes. Rebecca passed away the year after on 2 February and Wood died four years later on 24 August 1951. They were both buried in Portslade Cemetery. The kerbstone has long since gone, but the open book-style memorial remains, although much discoloured by the passage of time. When he died Wood had eighteen grandchildren and sixteen great-grandchildren.

Wood seems to have been enough of a celebrity for his portrait to be painted. One portrait is supposed to hang over the fireplace of HMS *Vincent* in Portsmouth, while another hangs in the wardroom of HMS *Excellent*, Whale Island, Portsmouth, having been presented to Commander Allan Adair. Then in August 2002 a portrait of Wood came up for auction. Irish artist Arthur David McCormick painted it in the 1890s and it is a fine and sensitive portrait. It was expected to fetch between £7,000 and £10,000, but in the event a telephone bidder secured it for an astonishing £22,325. A spokeswoman for auctioneers Bonhams said, 'It is an impressive price, but it's a very nice painting and quite large.'

Thomas Huntley Wood beside his wife's grave in the north-west part of Portslade Cemetery, 1947. (Buck)

24

Alan Osborne

& the Portslade Girl Pipers

Alan Osborne was born in March 1929 at 15 Shelldale Crescent, Portslade. His mother's side of the family had solid roots in Portslade and Alan's great-grandparents, Alfred and Esther Steele, lived in Crown Villa, an old house in Old Shoreham Road, which in their day was known as 22 Western Road. Crown Villa was built on such a narrow site that there was no space for a hall downstairs, and upstairs you had to go through one bedroom in order to reach the other one. The house has since been demolished. Esther's father was Abraham Peters, market gardener, and the family lived in Alma Cottage in Portslade Village, which is still there. His sons also worked as market gardeners, while their daughter Annie (Alan's grandmother) married a Mr Weller. The Weller children were Grace, Nellie (Alan's mother) and Arthur who was a great pal of Cecil Peters – also featured in this book. Mr Weller worked at Portslade Gas Works, but died of tuberculosis while still in his thirties. Annie's second husband was a Mr Witten.

Alan's paternal line came from Islington in London. The reason for the move south was because Alan's father was once stationed in the military camp sited in the grounds of Windlesham House School and rather liked the area. Alan's paternal grandmother, christened Mary Ann but known to all as Polly, had ten children. Her first marriage produced Clarence, Maud, Ernest, Stan, Ada and Charlie. After she was widowed she married a Mr Woodward and gave birth to Albert, Sid, Doris and Lennie. Clarence, who so disliked his name that he was called Fred, was sent to Russia with the British Army at the time of the revolution and was captured by the Bolsheviks. He ended up working in a Siberian salt mine, but was released in 1918. He lived at a number of addresses in Portslade, including Trafalgar Road and North Road. Polly lived at 1 Vale Road, next to Baker's, the wholesale tobacconist.

Alan's immediate family was more modest in size; his siblings were Eileen, Donald and Alma, who all went to school in Portslade. In 1947 Alan was called up for National Service, and to his surprise he was drafted to the Cameronians (Scottish Rifles). But he enjoyed the experience and certainly cut a dashing figure in his kilt. It also gave him a love of bagpipe music, which is how he came to form the Portslade Girl Pipers in 1973. At that time he lived in Abinger Villa, a large old house at 87 Abinger Road, where there was plenty of room for the girls to practise their pipes

*Alfred Steele married Esther Peters, daughter of Abraham Peters, market gardener, on
19 August 1871 at St Nicolas's Church, Portslade. They went on to have many children.
Alfred and Esther are seated in the centre, next to Esther is Annie (Alan Osborne's
grandmother), while next to Alfred is Charlotte. The sons in the back row, left to right, are
Alfred, Albert, Frederick and Henry. The small children in front are Edith and William.
That leaves three daughters unaccounted for – one of them was Henrietta, but the names of
the other two cannot be recalled. (Osborne)*

*Members of the Order of Buffaloes outside the George Inn, Portslade, photographed by H.W. Tubb
in the 1930s. Ernest Arthur Osborne (Alan's father) is seated third from the left. (Osborne)*

The dedication ceremony of Portslade War Memorial outside the British Legion Club in Trafalgar Road, 2 November 1930. In 1956 it was removed to Easthill Park. (Osborne)

Donald, Alma, Alan and Eileen Osborne in the back garden of 13 Gladstone Road, Portslade, 1932. (Osborne)

Silver Jubilee celebrations in Gladstone Road, 1936. (Osborne)

Alan Osborne in the Cameronians, 1947. (Osborne)

and to store instruments and uniform. The uniform consisted of a kilt in Dress Gordon tartan with a green jacket and lace jabot. Alan obtained permission for the girls to wear the Gordon badge on their Glengarry hats and the Cameronian badge on their plaids. Their first public performance was on New Year's Eve 1973. Afterwards they gave regular performances both at private functions and at public events such as Hove Lions' Day at Hove Park. They were always much in demand at the New Year and on Burns Night. A highlight for the Pipers was when they were part of the youth parade to celebrate the Queen's Silver Jubilee in 1977 and marched past Buckingham Palace. There were also trips to Ireland and Holland. At its height the band could muster forty-three girls, but they were not all bagpipers at that stage as some of them played bell lyres. The band broke up in about 1983.

Alan's father became a window cleaner in 1919 and Alan followed in his footsteps, finally hanging up his bucket in October 2003. But his son Gary continues to work as a window cleaner, and he is a familiar sight in the Boundary Road and Station Road area. So far the family have been cleaning windows for eighty-five years. Alan was the first in the area to use the new-fangled squeegee imported from the USA (the familiar rubber-bladed instrument). Other men in the trade had a good laugh, but when they saw how efficient it was they were soon demanding to know where to get one.

Portslade Girl Pipers outside the Metropole Hotel, August 1977. Left to right: Claire Middleton, Vicky Funnell and Lorraine Sutton. (Author)

25

Norman Daniel Shaw

of Shaw's Stores

Daniel Shaw set up shop at Hove in 1862. His father worked a barge on the River Ouse at Lewes, but Daniel opted to work as a grocer – a trade in which other members of the family were engaged in various parts of Sussex. The shop he chose was on the corner of George Street, which in those days consisted almost entirely of artisans' dwellings. The shop's correct address was 11/12 Church Street, Cliftonville – Cliftonville being the name of a new development consisting of Osborne Villas, Medina Villas, Albany Villas, St Catherine's Terrace, Ventnor Villas, Hova Villas and George Street. The land east of Cliftonville was undeveloped as far as the Brunswick area; likewise the land west of Hove Street was farmland up to the Portslade border. At the time the population of Hove was just over 9,000. There was a field used by lads for cricket on what was to become the Town Hall site. There was no through road to Brighton along the present Church Road/Western Road, and after Cliftonville horse-drawn traffic had to go down to the seafront road.

One of the first things Daniel Shaw did was to make a record of his customers' purchases. In the interests of economy he did not buy a readymade day-book, but made up one of his own. This he did by using a trade card advertising Field's Night Lights, which he folded so that the blue coloured cardboard faced inwards. Then lined ledger paper was sewn into this cover. Here in neat copper-plate handwriting he recorded the daily trade with a satisfied 'Paid' at the end of every ruled space. His busiest time of year was in high summer. You might think this was due to an influx of holiday makers, but in reality it was itinerant workers arriving to help with harvest and sheep-shearing at local farms who provided the extra trade.

Daniel Shaw made an imposing shopkeeper with his thick, bushy beard and a crisp white apron of such generous proportions that his shoes were barely visible beneath it. The words 'Cheesemonger and Butterman' were emblazoned above his shop front. The beautiful brass scales and large scoop used in the shop in later years were carefully preserved and became family heirlooms, which I saw in 1990. There was also a delicate pair of tea-tasting scales that packed away neatly into their own box.

The story is still told in the family of the plumber who sent Daniel Shaw a bill in the 1890s itemising work carried out such as fixing the taps. The various items of labour were summarised by an amusing but comprehensive item 'and humbugging

Daniel Shaw stands in the entrance to his shop, c. 1870. *(Shaw)*

about'. It was a tradition in the Shaw family that a son of each generation should have the Christian name of Daniel. Thus Daniel's son was Alfred Daniel, his grandson was Norman Daniel and his great-grandson is Edmund Daniel. All four generations bearing the name Daniel were involved in the running of the shop at Hove.

As his father had done before him, Alfred Daniel Shaw lived above the shop, which by then was numbered as 153/155 Church Road, Hove, and became known as Shaw's Stores. The premises were still rented from Miss Gallard, daughter of George Gallard, one of the developers of Cliftonville. There is a photograph of A.D. Shaw in 1917 wearing an imposing chain of office as President of the Brighton, Hove & District Grocers and Provision Merchants Association (see page 126).

When St Dunstan's Pearson House, the home for blind soldiers, was founded in Kemp Town, Brighton, in 1918 the Association raised money to furnish it, and for very many years gave a Christmas party and arranged summer outings for local St Dunstaners. Another reminder of the First World War is a bleak little certificate dated 1917 issued to A.D. Shaw by the Ministry of Food, registering him as an official retailer of sugar.

Both of A.D. Shaw's sons were born above the shop. Norman Daniel arrived in 1905, six years after his brother Herbert Alfred, who eventually entered the legal profession. Their mother, Martha Ann (Annie) Shaw, looked after the children, and there was a live-in maid to help with the chores. George Street in those days was a real little community. The artisans' cottages gradually gave way to a street of small

Alfred Daniel Shaw, 1917. (Shaw)

shops and all the shopkeepers knew each other, as they did in Church Road too.

It is surprising the number of grocery businesses there were – Hunter, thought to be the earliest (now Cullen's), Humphrey (later Teetgen, then Unwins wine merchants) and Upperton in the next block – all on the south side of Church Road. William Upperton and Alfred Shaw were school and lifelong friends; they were competitors on either side of Church Road (120 and 153), but they later became partners at 189 Church Road as Warcus Stores. At one time they contemplated having a van with Upperton painted on one side, Shaw on the other and Warcus at the back, but the idea never materialised. James Lee had a grocery shop in George Street and there was a host of other multiple grocers such as Worlds, Pearks, Maypole, Lipton and Sainsbury, while Home & Colonial had a place in Blatchington Road. Norman remembered going to Marks & Spencer's Penny Bazaar in George Street.

As a young boy Norman watched the lamp-lighter doing his rounds, which included the gas lamp at the foot of George Street; another memory was of the three street musicians who used to play their brass instruments on the corner of George Street and Church Road, outside the men's outfitters shop later known as Broadley's. There was a blacksmith's forge in George Street where he watched the sparks fly as the blacksmith worked, and another one on the seafront on a site now occupied by the King Alfred.

Norman remembered the cinema in George Street with its ornate façade. Unfortunately, he never saw the inside, because his mother was afraid of the risk of infection. She also thought that the popular nickname 'flea-pit' might prove to be too accurate for comfort. Mr Lewonski owned the cinema, he also happened to be the local funeral director. As befitted his more sombre profession, he was always dressed rather soberly, but no doubt gave his cinema patrons a warm welcome. Hove fire station was still in George Street in the 1920s and the Hove coat-of-arms adorning the building can still be seen today. The fire engine was still pulled by horses. There was great excitement when a new motor Merryweather fire engine gave a demonstration on the seafront. Norman was one of those who flocked to see this spectacle.

An event he did not see – much to his annoyance – was the annual procession when the circus came to town. This was because it always seemed to coincide with the family holiday in the Sussex countryside. But his father, who commuted by rail between Hove and the holiday home, would thoughtfully compile a list of all the animals and artists in the procession so that Norman would know exactly what he had missed.

The circus camped out in Wish Meadow near Aldrington Recreation Ground, popularly called Wish Park.

Norman fondly recalled the horse buses and he enjoyed kneeling at the front inside window to watch the backs of the horses jogging up and down with tails swishing. Inside the bus, seats ran the whole length with passengers seated facing each other. The top deck was open, which was lovely in hot weather but miserable in the rain. These seats faced to the front and if they were already wet, despite the apron-like coverings, it was best to remain standing, facing backwards. At roughly the half-way stage, passengers from Hove to Brighton, would hear the conductor call, 'York Road – end of the penny fares.' At the time some motor buses were running as well as the electric (battery powered) ones.

It all meant a hardy type of existence and Norman remembered how much walking people did, even quite young children.

On Sunday afternoons and on Wednesday half-day closing, the family would take a nice long walk for recreation with destinations such as West Blatchington to look at Farmer Brown's crops and the windmill; Hangleton, which was farmed by the Hardwicks to watch the ducks in the pond by the Manor House; the Droveway where King's Farm, later Hole's, was to be found; the Three Cornered Copse at the top of Woodland Drive and St Ann's Well Gardens.

In the summer the Shaws had an umbrella tent on the beach at West Hove. These contraptions were popular because they enabled people to change into or out of their swimming costumes while still preserving their modesty. The costumes, even for young boys, were baggy woollen affairs with wide straps over the shoulders. Norman also went to the old Hove Baths – the larger one for men was on a site now occupied by

Bath Court and the smaller one for ladies was west of Victoria Cottages. He also visited Brill's Baths in East Street, Brighton, which had a refinement on the traditional way of being taught to swim – being thrown in at the deep end. The device was a wire and pulley contraption stretched across the baths to support the would-be swimmer which would prevent him from drowning before he had learnt how to swim.

To be able to ballroom dance was considered a social refinement. Accordingly, Norman was despatched to dancing classes in Ventnor Villas. Miss Gladys Toye was the energetic instructor and she started to teach at the age of sixteen. Miss Toye eventually became part of the Shaw family by marrying Norman's brother Herbert. Her father (another Daniel as it happens) was manager of W. Miles & Company, the fruit, flower and vegetable shop, which enjoyed what was termed the carriage trade. A lady would draw

Norman in his sailor suit, 1911. (Shaw)

Children in George Street near Freeman, Hardy & Willis's shoe shop, c. *1910. Festoons of shoes can be seen hanging on the right. (Flowers)*

James Lee's grocery shop at 39 George Street lasted from 1886 to the 1930s. (Jeeves)

George Street with Hove fire station on the left, 1914. (Brighton & Hove Libraries)

The pond at Hangleton Manor. (Jeeves)

Umbrella tents on the beach at west Hove, 1912. You could pitch your tent for free on the beach opposite Langdale Gardens. Tents had to be taken down not later than one hour after sunset. (Author)

up outside the establishment in her carriage and the shopkeeper would come out and take down her order. On one occasion Daniel Toye forgot his subordinate status and rested his foot on the step near the carriage door while he wrote down the order. Nothing was said, but the lady's withering glance made him remove his foot hurriedly.

In 1923 Norman Shaw joined his father in business. It seemed to act as a spur to the enterprise, because soon it expanded. By this time Alfred had bought the original shop from the Gallard Estate and the premises were extended northwards, first by taking over a greengrocer's shop in George Street, then the umbrella and hairdressing shop next to it. In 1928 Norman won first prize in the final examinations of the Institute of Certified Grocers and the celebrations included an outing for all the staff. (Later on two employees, Walter Payne and Roy Pettyfer, also won major prizes in the final examination of the Grocers' Institute – the latter with the first prize exactly twenty years after his employer's triumph). There was another celebrated staff outing when Norman married Margaret Shemeld in 1933.

In 1934 a new type of shop window was installed, the first in the area. It was known as invisible glass, and was curved in such a way that a customer looking in would not be aware that there was any glass at all. Shaw's Stores was very conscious of the appeal that good window dressing could exercise, and won prizes for their displays promoting various grocery items.

All this changed during the Second World War, as all the windows were boarded up for safety in 1940, although part of the wooden shutters could be hinged open during the daytime. Staff shortages led Shaw's to make a daring innovation – self-service – in fact they were pioneers in this field in the area. But life for both staff and customers was difficult during the war years because of the shortages. Norman collected cartoons printed in newspapers on the subject of rationing and shortages. One of them showed a manager saying to his assistant, 'Remember . . . to casual customers "No", to regulars "Sorry, no", and to special regulars, "Terribly sorry, no"'. After the war customers expected service to return to the way it had been in the 1930s and so self-service was out – but not for long. When Palmeira Stores closed down Shaw's bought up all their self-service fixtures. But Shaw's never lost their reputation for service with a smile.

In the 1950s eggs were still displayed in great wicker baskets from which they were sold loose. There was a restaurant upstairs and Mr Westerman, the builder, had a bright idea for improving customer appeal. He used part of a disused passage to create a log cabin for children with the legend 'Chuck House' above the door. Inside there were small chairs and tables.

Norman had become managing director of Shaw's Stores in 1937 on the death of his father, and in 1957 his elder son, Edmund Daniel Shaw, joined the firm. Edmund, the great-grandson of the founder, spent his two years of National Service in the Royal Army Ordnance Corps. He was trained at Eaton Hall Officer Cadet School and served in Singapore and Malaya during the Emergency. On his return, he retrained for the grocery trade with the well-known firm of Williamson & Tredgold in Bournemouth and worked with his father until 1960. He then received an attractive offer from Stewart Ltd of Upper Market Street, Hove – the South Coast Wholesalers and founders of VG (Voluntary Group). The family considered it too good an opportunity to miss. Like his father and grandfather, Edmund was

Shaw's Stores, c. 1936. (Shaw)

Shaw's Stores in wartime dress with a machine gun nest on the pavement opposite. The all-clear had just sounded. (Shaw)

elected President of Brighton Grocers' Association (Wholesale and Retail). He enjoyed a successful career, becoming Managing Director of Stewart's and later of other companies in the Wheatsheaf Group.

Music has always been an important interest for the family. Norman enjoyed a long and happy association with the Brighton & Hove Operatic Society as a well-remembered performer and also as chorus master, assistant conductor, vice-chairman, chairman of the publicity committee and finally life vice-president. From 1973 he was also president of the Gilbert & Sullivan Society (Sussex Branch). Norman's younger son, David Norman, gained an organ scholarship to Brasenose College, Oxford. He was on the music staff of Covent Garden Opera House for many years and conducted a number of performances. He has enjoyed many artistic appointments and musical assignments both in Britain and abroad.

In 1962 Shaw's Stores celebrated its centenary, the same year in which George Street won the Civic Award for its refurbishment, and was visited by the Queen and Prince Philip. In 1964 Norman Shaw retired and Shaw's Stores closed its doors for the last time. Many people expressed their regret and felt that Hove would never be the same again. But the whole style of shopping had changed irrevocably and was no longer a mix of necessity and social pleasure. Many of the staff gave long and loyal service, and Norman remembered them with gratitude and admiration for their hard work and cheerfulness.

In 1965 Norman's mother celebrated her 100th birthday. Norman also proved to be long-lived, but just missed his centenary. He died on 27 January 2004 at the Regent House Nursing Home, Hove, at the age of ninety-eight, by which time he was a grandfather and great-grandfather. His funeral was held on 9 February 2004, and afterwards there was a Service of Thanksgiving for his life at the Unitarian Church, New Road, Brighton.

26

The Woolgar Family

The Woolgars have a long association with the area. Perhaps the earliest mention of the family was John Woolgar who was elected headborough and ale-taster of Hove in 1568, 1569 and 1578, and in 1588 he was elected constable. In 1874 Thomas Woolgar was the registered boatman at Hove of *Golden Grove*, a 14ft rowing boat and *Sea Spray*, a 21ft sailing boat. Edgar Voysey owned both boats. But it was not long before the Woolgars came to own their own vessels. The Woolgars enjoyed taking part in local events such as regattas. In September 1887 Mr A. Woolgar won a prize in Brighton Waterman's Regatta in the class for yawls and luggers with his yawl *Sweetheart*, and in August 1892 at Hove Annual Regatta the Woolgars carried off two prizes sailing the yawl *Sweetheart* and the lugger *Maggie*.

The Woolgars' original pitch was at the bottom of Hove Street but after the promenade was altered their base was moved to the foot of First Avenue. In 1903 Messrs Woolgar & Minall protested to Hove Council that their old huts had been removed on council orders but their new boating station opposite First Avenue was not large enough. The council agreed to provide a hut not exceeding 20ft by 8ft for £5 a year. The boats took visitors out for a trip on the briny – the Woolgars at Hove while at Brighton Captain Collins took trippers out in his famous *Skylark*. To help those who were not used to scrambling aboard boats, a little trestle-type ladder was kept close at hand to enable pleasure seekers to climb into the boat without getting their feet wet. The Woolgars later moved into other beach activities by providing bathing machines in which people could change in privacy, and they also hired out towels and costumes.

Henry Woolgar was born in the 1880s and was known to one and all as Harry. He joined the Merchant Navy and once worked aboard the famous *Cutty Sark*. In Bristol he met a young lady called Amelia whom he promised to marry on returning from his voyage. But it was seven long years before he arrived back to claim her hand, as he had jumped ship in Australia. But Amelia was still patiently waiting for him. The couple married and had two children, and by 1905 were living at 5 Beach Cottages. Harry was a bit of a character and cultivated his Old Salt image. He was rarely seen without his nautical headgear and pipe and he sported a beard. He was popular with visiting children and knew how to entertain sightseers. Sometimes he would appear with an octopus, which he allowed to climb up his arm with its tentacles to gasps of horror from onlookers. The octopus was delivered courtesy of

Beach Cottages were relics of Old Hove south of the coast road (later called Kingsway). They were built in about 1813. The King Alfred complex now covers the site. (Brighton & Hove Libraries)

local fishermen who sometimes found an octopus in the summer months lodged on top of a lobster pot, having sucked all the goodness out of the lobster.

Also sharing the Woolgar household was a pet monkey called Jacko brought back by his son William Charles Woolgar from a trip to West Africa while serving in the

Merchant Navy aboard the cable ship *Collona*. One day when the family was out, Jacko pulled the tablecloth off the table thereby upsetting the paraffin lamp and setting fire to the house. The monkey escaped, somewhat singed, and the family moved to no. 2. Another family pet was Ponto the dog, who by all accounts was a great character and always much in evidence in family photographs. He used to carry Harry's dinner from Beach Cottages to the bathing station.

In 1913 a note in Council Minutes stated that the bathing machines owned by Woolgar & Son and other owners were stored on the foreshore at the Wish during the winter. In 1921 Woolgar & Son of 2 Beach Cottages held licences for twenty-one bathing machines and T. & H. Woolgar of 3 Beach Cottages held a licence for a rowing boat. In 1926 all bathing machines and bathing tents at

Harry Woolgar and Charlie Woolgar with Ponto the dog, c. 1921. (Woolgar)

Harry Woolgar is holding Ponto and Charlie Woolgar is on the right. The old-fashioned bathing machines had large wheels to prevent them sinking in the shingle. (Woolgar)

The seafront is strewn with wreckage after a storm, but the stout bathing machine survived – by this time it was used as an office. (Woolgar)

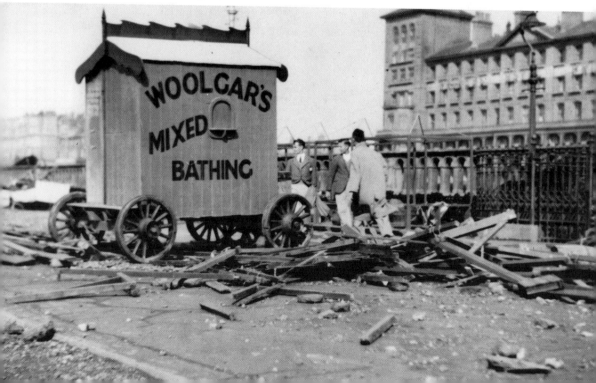

Violet Reed, sister-in-law of Jerry Woolgar, in the garden of 22 Hove Street. (Woolgar)

Hove were inspected and found to be satisfactory, except for the machines belonging to H. Woolgar & Son who kept twenty opposite First Avenue. Their attention was drawn to the 'dilapidated appearance' of the machines. Some attempt had been made to remedy the defects, as more of the machines had been fitted with low wheels instead of the old-fashioned large wheels. Mr Woolgar promised to reduce the number each year. But the large wheels were there for a purpose – they stopped the machine from sinking into the shingle.

Harry and Amelia Woolgar christened their daughter Amelia, after her mother, and their son William Charles. While the son did not mind his Christian names as such, he was deeply grieved that his initials should spell WC, and consequently he was always known as Jerry. He was born on 7 December 1905 and in 1928 married Daisy Reed, whose sisters were also blessed with flower names – Violet and Lily. The couple moved to Osborne Villas while Harry moved to Sussex Road. Jerry's son, William Henry, was almost a birthday present for his father, as he was born on 1 December 1930. At some stage the family moved to 22 Hove Street, an old flint cottage on the corner of Vallance Gardens.

In the 1920s Jerry Woolgar owned two boats – the *Leader* (a sailing boat) and the *Princess* (a motor boat) and the latter was his first motor boat. Both vessels were based on Hove beach. The next boat he owned was the *Four Winds*, which was 24ft long and had an engine. She was built in 1930 and was sold in 1948. The replacement was the *Phoebe Hessell*, built at the Lady Bee Yard, Southwick. Unfortunately, she had to go two years later, as it proved impossible to keep up the mortgage repayments from the small amount of money she earned.

Bathing tents became popular in the later 1920s and 1930s, and those fronting the beach were in constant use. But there were also tents at the back marked 'Strictly Private'. Young Bill Woolgar, Harry's grandson, was told never to disturb the occupants. Courting couples were wont to hire these tents for the afternoon. When war was declared in 1939 Hove beaches were cleared and all the gear, tents, floats

Charlie and Harry Woolgar meet the toffs – Sir Cooper and Lady Rawson. Sir Cooper Rawson was the local Conservative MP from 1922 to 1944, and in the 1931 election his majority was 62,253, an all-time record. (Woolgar)

The Leader *with Harry Woolgar and Charlie, c. 1921. (Woolgar)*

The Princess *on Hove Beach. (Woolgar)*

A view from Courtenay Gate showing Woolgar's Bathing Station with pleasure boats drawn up on the beach. (Woolgar)

and bathing machines were stored in garages in Namrick Mews for the duration. Afterwards the machines were sold off to Lytham St Anne's.

The *Brighton & Hove Gazette* (12 March 1949) carried an article on the activities of William Woolgar of Medina Place, Hove. Apparently he had a monopoly on catching sand fleas or sand hoppers, which he pursued all the year round along the coast stretching from Rye to Littlehampton. When caught, the tiny shrimp-like crustaceans were packed in tins and sold for £1 a pint. But it took thousands of them to make up a pint – they stayed alive for around three or four days. Mr Woolgar's customers were London Zoo and Brighton Aquarium where the creatures provided live food for marine exhibits, particularly sea anemones. The family remembered that his unusual occupation resulted in his appearance on the popular radio show *In Town Tonight* in 1937.

In 1952 Harry Woolgar died and in 1958 his grandson W.H. Woolgar, Shoreham Local Fisheries Officer, reported that shrimp catchers (push net and trawl) had complained of pollution at low-water mark in an area bounded by Seaside Villas in Western Esplanade and Brighton Power Station. The oily substance appeared to come from a pipe south of the Gas Works.

27

John Bryon

Childhood Days at Hove

John Bryon was born in 1925 in Montgomery Street, not many doors down from the Eclipse pub. He was not the only child in the family, but his two half-brothers and two half-sisters were much older. They had all been born or had grown up in the same house. His father, Edward Bryon, was partially sighted and earned his living as a piano tuner. Indeed he was at the top of his profession and tuned the instrument at the Dome for such great pianists as Solomon, Dame Myra Hess, and the Australian Eileen Joyce – on the occasion of his ninetieth birthday in 1967 the latter sent him a greetings telegram. He remembered Myra Hess being particularly fussy about the height of the piano stool, which she liked to be at a lower level than most pianists preferred. Once she suggested that staff cut a couple of inches off the legs. He also tuned the piano when Dame Clara Butt came to sing. The celebrated Austrian tenor Richard Tauber strode about the stage while Bryon was at work on the piano, warming up by singing 'Mares eat oats and does eat oats'. Edward Byron had a light baritone voice that he used to good effect by singing in the choir of Holy Cross Church, Shelley Road, Hove. He was born in North Wales and moved to Hove in 1897 to join the staff at Lyon & Hall's in Western Road, Brighton. His second wife had been a nurse in Devon before their marriage, and in the days before the National Health Service neighbours would frequently call on her for advice and help.

The area around Montgomery Street was a self-contained little community and neighbours were on friendly terms. The streets were full of life – the children often played outside because there was not much traffic to worry about. The muffin man called regularly with his tray of muffins, ringing his bell as he walked to alert customers. Another itinerant trader (John never did learn his name) pushed an old pram around containing a variety of goods including cotton reels, lace and handcream. At every door he called out 'Cold cream, Vaseline, Melrose'. Fresh fish could be purchased from the man with the barrow and there were visits from traders delivering bread, meat and vegetables to the door. Indeed the housewife had no need to stagger home laden with shopping, as deliveries were the norm. Goods would arrive by horse and cart, handcart or trade bike.

In the late afternoon and early evening the streets would reverberate with the call of the newsboy selling copies of the *Evening Argus*. Then it was time for the

The Bryon family, 1927. From left to right: May, Frank, Mr Bryon, Bob, Elizabeth and Mrs Bryon holding John. (Bryon)

lamplighter to arrive. John remembers him as a skilful bicycle rider, riding his steed like a knight of old on his war horse, holding his long pole like a lance. In this manner he would ride up to each lamppost and with a dextrous twist of the pole, light up the lamp without having to dismount. On Sundays the Salvation Army Band sometimes played hymn tunes standing grouped on the street corner, and quite often there would be visiting bands of unemployed Welsh miners who raised desperately needed funds by singing. On Tuesdays there was more music provided by a man who trundled his heavy player piano around on wheels and churned out popular tunes. John remembered a blind beggar who stood near the railway bridge in Sackville Road to beg. When he heard a heavy footstep approaching, he would discreetly turn his outstretched hand inwards, in case the boots belonged to a policeman.

As well as numerous corner shops, there were many small shops in George Street and Blatchington Road close at hand. The aroma of Wilshers, the grocers, at the top of George Street, lingered in John's memory. It was compounded of dried fruit and tea, salty bacon and cheese. Of course this was in the days before pre-packaging when the housewife bought her staples such as rice and sugar loose and the shopkeeper poured out the required amount into paper cones. At Maypole's, half-way down on the left, you could watch white-coated assistants cutting the butter and patting it into shape with wooden implements. The shop specialised in dairy produce, bacon and ham. The best time for bargain shopping as far as food was concerned was late on Saturday night when shopkeepers needed to get rid of their perishables and so lowered the price. In this way John's brothers once purchased seven herrings for 6*d* and 1lb of cherries for 3*d*.

The Co-op in Blatchington Road was a fascinating place for children because of the overhead wires running from the various counters to the cash desk. When you purchased an item, your money and bill were enclosed in a small brass canister and off it whizzed to the cash desk. You had to wait patiently until you saw it zooming back again with your change inside. It was the latest technology in customer care at the time!

Edward Bryon, piano tuner. (Bryon)

As for a small boy's pocket money – there was a wealth of choice in the sweet line for a modest sum. For ½*d* or even ¼*d* you could buy sweets such as liquorice sticks or liquorice root, gobstoppers and aniseed balls, toffee apples and those funny little chewy tiger nuts. A comic would set you back ½*d* or 1*d*. When you felt rich there were two picture palaces to choose from – one in Haddington Street and the other in George Street. They put on special matinees for children and it only cost a few pence to get in.

Most of the houses in Montgomery Street did not have the luxury of a bathroom and bath time involved a walk to the Public Baths in Livingstone Road armed with your own towel and bar of soap. Of course the Baths would provide both these items, but it all added to the cost. The bath tubs were in separate cubicles and the system was designed to prevent a person from using more than his fair share of hot water – there were no taps that the user could turn on and off. If you needed more hot or cold water you had to call your request out to the attendant.

As everything was close at hand, children did not need to go far from their own neighbourhood. There were plenty of buses, but the cost of a bus ticket only added to the strain on the family budget. The other option was to walk everywhere. It is instructive to note that even a modest walk as far as Hangleton was held to be a great novelty. Once under the railway bridge and heading towards the old church, it was like being in a different world, because it was all countryside then with only a couple of houses in view. On rare occasions the family took the train from Aldrington Halt to Devil's Dyke, but mostly the children stood by the fence to watch the trains trundle by.

John attended Connaught Road Infants' School first of all, followed by a spell at Ellen Street Junior School. Discipline was strict at Ellen Street, and Mr Lloyd in particular would not stand for any nonsense. His readiness to wield his short, thick cane was proverbial. He had a short, bull-like neck and curiously did not wear socks. Mr Lloyd joined the school as a temporary stand-in during the First World War but, unhappily for the children, he stayed permanently.

When he was eleven, John had the novelty of being among the first batch of boys to go to the newly established Hove County School for Boys in Nevill Road. Everything was brand new and the masters were a fine bunch, although naturally the boys were still ruled with a rod of iron. Mr Tarbrett (nicknamed Tabby of course) enjoyed such an awesome reputation that he only had to clear his throat for all the boys to fall silent immediately. Mr Norden was headmaster and claimed to read only the Bible and *The Times*, but in fact he was a cultured Cambridge man. Mr Thorpe taught French so well that he inspired young John with a love of the language that has never left him. Another lifelong interest he acquired was a talent for science, which led to a career in chemistry. (In the 1960s he was engaged in research work on abrasives for a London firm.) An event that stands out in his memory from about the time he started at Hove County School was the sight of the Zeppelin *Hindenburg* flying majestically over Hove on the evening of 5 July 1936. Thousands witnessed the event, because the roar of engines brought people outside to see what was happening. The Zeppelin was flying at a height of 3,000ft. On 3 May 1937 the *Hindenburg* exploded, killing thirty-six of the ninety-seven passengers at the US Naval Station in Lakehurst, New Jersey. It had been thought that helium gas was the culprit, but recent theories point to the type of paint used on the outer covering.

John's grandma, Mrs Hutson, was a remarkable woman. She ran a girls' training home – in fact she was the matron. The establishment went under the title of the Hove Training Home for Girls. It was a charitable institution in which poor girls were trained in the domestic arts. An advertisement in the *Hove Parish Magazine* for June 1892 ran thus: 'Ladies will greatly assist in this useful and good work by applying for Servants, etc, at the above Institution, where there are a number of

The Co-op in Blatchington Road opened in 1920. (Author)

Hove County School for Boys cost £45,000 to build and was formally opened on 28 October 1936. (Brighton & Hove Libraries)

names on the Registers, and a lady is in daily attendance to give all necessary information.' The Home was at 83 Goldstone Villas, but in 1892 a new one opened in Clarendon Road. The magazine continued,

> On Monday, May 9th, the new Hove Girls' Training Home at 41 Clarendon Villas was opened with a short but most impressive Service by the Vicar. . . . But previous to the religious ceremony, an interesting and pretty scene took place in the large Class-room. After all the visitors had taken their seats, the girls, with bright and happy faces and most neatly dressed, came in, and were no sooner arranged in their places when they were followed by the Matron, Mrs Hutson, and her youngest child, the latter presenting to Mrs Peacey (the vicar's wife) in the name of the girls, a most lovely bouquet of choice flowers, while the Matron handed to the Vicar the following Address – The Matron and girls of the Training Home, both past and present, wish to express to Mr and Mrs Peacey and all the ladies who have taken such continued, kind and earnest interest in their welfare, both temporal and spiritual, the deep sense of their gratitude, and take this opportunity for showing their thankfulness by giving themselves the pleasure of contributing their small but hearty offerings towards a useful present to the Home. They are, however, fully aware that the best way to show their true gratitude for all the kindness they daily receive, is to try with all their hearts to be good, honest, industrious girls.

John's brother Frank went to East Hove School in Holland Road. It was a busy site with the electricity works over the road, the ice works in Holland Road and a church and a pub on opposite corners – needless to say, the pub is the only one to survive to this day. Anyway, a standard Hove joke was to call the area the 'Four Nations' because of the four institutions on the corners – that is education, electrification, salvation and damnation with refrigeration not far off. In 1917 Frank started work at Lyon & Hall, Western Road, Brighton – both he and his brother Lawrence (Bob) had trained as piano tuners. At first Frank's wages were only 5*s* a week. But when fully trained at the end of five years he was earning 18*s*. The brothers served in the Armed Forces during the Second World War with Bob taking part in the Normandy Landings. Their sisters married Welsh brothers and went to live at Rhyl. Before marriage Elizabeth was a typist at Cox & Barnard's, the stained-glass firm, while May was in service.

28

Arthur Henry Collins

Working on the Hove Echo

Arthur's father was a reader who worked on *The Times* – the position of reader being a much-prized white-collar job. In the 1890s the family decided to take a three-year lease on 52 Portland Road, Hove, although Mr Collins remained in London staying with Uncle Tom and only visited Hove at weekends. It was not much of a visit, because he arrived at breakfast time on Saturday and spent most of the rest of the day catching up on his sleep – then he caught the teatime train back to London on Sunday. He had promised to find a job in Brighton when they moved, but somehow he never quite had the nerve to make a break with Fleet Street. Meanwhile, Mrs Collins built up a good little business by letting rooms to holiday-makers, many of whom were friends or relatives or had connections with the printing trade. She would cater for two families who had separate apartments. The rent included all cooking, but the guests purchased their own food. For two weeks in the summer the house was given over to board-residence, which meant that some fourteen or fifteen people sat down to their meals at the family table with Mrs Collins, Will, Arthur and their sister Dolly.

Meanwhile, Arthur had decided not to return to school and soon found a job at Lewonski's in George Street earning 5s a week – the hours were from 8 a.m. to 6 p.m. Arthur described Mr Lewonski as having 'a mane of black hair and fierce handle-bar moustache'. He thought he was Polish in origin. Mr Lewonski ran a large furniture store as well as being an undertaker's furnisher. Arthur's duties included dusting the shop every morning. At the back there was a huge warehouse crammed full of bedding, mattresses and pillows. Sometimes he would be sent out with a man to help him lay linoleum. Arthur also ran errands, delivered goods by handcart, and looked after an incubator holding 500 eggs. The eggs had to be damped with a wet cloth and turned every day. After three weeks or so the chicks would hatch and were transferred to a drying box. Later they were taken to the premises where the coffins were made and the stables situated, to be reared by a foster mother. Mr Lewonski was obviously a man of parts, because he later became the proprietor of the cinema in George Street, added the career of estate agent to his talents and went on to become a Hove councillor.

Arthur stayed at Lewonski's for six months, as he took another job at the grocer's a few doors down in George Street at 8s a week for the same hours. He soon became acquainted with the gentle art of 'fiddling'. It worked like this. The proprietor would visit large houses to talk to the cook and if the cook agreed to buy all groceries from him he would make sure a bonus of £1 a month was forthcoming. He clawed the money back by under supplying all the butter, fats, tea, fruit, rice and so on despatched to the house would be a little short of the amount ordered.

In March 1899 Arthur followed his father's footsteps into the printing trade. Arthur commented that his father was not blessed with foresight, because it was obvious that soon newspapers would be set by machinery. Even at *The Times* there was a machine to set up printer's type as well as a Linotype, an American machine that could cast a line of type on one 'slug'. But it was decided that Arthur should learn the commercial side, that is newspaper setting. His mother took the matter in hand and together they visited every printer in Brighton and Hove. Her line of patter was the same in each establishment, that he was bound to make a good 'comp' because he played the piano so well. Although her remark was met by a superior smile it turned out to be true. He was taken on at Emery's, which was situated on the corner of Vallance Road and Church Road – today estate agents Mishon Mackay occupy the ground floor while Stonelands School of Dancing and the Theatre Arts have the upper floors. Elmutt Clifton and his brother ran the business in the two communicating shops – one was a newsagent and stationer, while the other was given over to the printing works with machines on the ground floor and the compositing departments on the upper floor. Here the *Hove Echo* was produced.

The foreman's name was Dyer, and although an able man he was an exacting taskmaster. The team of comps was extremely skilful, and Arthur had to admit that he never saw better designs or workmanship anywhere else. Mr Dyer said Arthur was sure to be worth something at the end of his month's trial, but he received no pay for that month. Afterwards he was put on piecework, but he earned nothing for the first 100 lines and 1s for every 100 after. He never discovered why he was not paid for the first 100 lines. There was another boy in the office, who was a boarder and he also earned nothing for his first 100 lines, but that was to pay for his board and lodging. This did not apply to Arthur who still lived at home. Despite that, Arthur was happy there and worked with two journeymen in the top room with a marvellous view over the churchyard to the Downs in the distance. In his first week Arthur managed to set 500 lines, much to Mr Dyer's astonishment. The boarding boy never managed to exceed this amount and received 4s on pay-day. However, Arthur gradually increased his speed by 50 to 100 lines a week, until after six months he could do 2,100 or 2,200 lines a week.

Mr Dyer was less than delighted at his prowess because he had not bargained on such an increase in wages, and so he set about trying to reduce his output and thus his pay. He would call Arthur down to help on the cutting machine for an hour or so (no pay of course) or hold copy for the editor (no pay again). But he still managed to keep to his 2,100 mark. Then he was given the chore of collecting the London newspapers from the 8.15 a.m. train at Brighton – again no pay – or on Fridays when the *Hove Echo* was published he was told to take parcels of it to a newsagent in Brighton, which was at least 3 miles away and he went on foot. It is pleasant to

There was a fire at Emery's on 9 July 1913. Some books from Hove Library, sent for rebinding, were lost. (Jeeves)

record that in fact Mr Dyer was doing Arthur a favour by making him faster and faster at his work, until he became what was known as a 'whip' in the trade; that is he could do twice as much work as was expected of a man, as laid down by the trade union. He kept up his speed throughout his career, and in later years he could even go as fast as a machine could, that is six lines a minute. All the time he was learning how to punctuate correctly, polish up his spelling and widen his general knowledge.

He also became a reporter for the *Hove Echo* as a freelance just for the love of the thing. But of course there were perks, particularly when he attended the lavish banquets held at Hove Town Hall. He would receive a wonderful meal for nothing and reported the proceedings in full. It might have been useful if he had known shorthand, but it did not bother him, because he had an exceptional memory and was able to remember all that had gone on and report it faithfully. The only thing he had to ensure was that he knew the name and status of any speaker. He enjoyed turning up at other events such as football matches, tennis tournaments, swimming events, polo matches, concerts, entertainments and especially the circuses, which became a great love of his. It was a matter of great satisfaction that the editor seldom altered his copy.

Arthur made one friend at Emery's – the foreman's son. Every day between early April and late September they would go straight from work for a swim. There was a free bathing station for men only close at hand. They were young and daring and must have been good swimmers too. It was a point of honour to them that they must swim out further than any other man who might be bathing at the same time. As there were frequently policemen from the convalescent home who were keen swimmers, this sometimes meant a lengthy excursion. Looking back some sixty years on, Arthur shuddered to think how far out they swam and they would even sometimes go in when the red flag was flying.

In 1900 the Collins family decided to return to London and Arthur Collins did not visit Hove again until fifty-five years later.

29

Joyce Hopkins

Old Hove Street

The Hopkins family moved from Portsmouth to Hove in about 1925 when Joyce was eight years old. Her father was a marine photographer, and although her mother was born and bred in Portsmouth she did not wish to stay there. At first the family lodged with some old friends in Westbourne Street while their house in Hove Street was being constructed. It was called Wokingham Lodge and was afterwards numbered 42 Hove Street. At the back there was a large greenhouse where Mr and Mrs Hopkins nurtured their prize carnations. In fact he was so particular that he would even get up in the middle of the night to check on the temperature in the run up to the flower show. The Brighton, Hove & Sussex Horticultural Society put on a Summer Show at the Corn Exchange and the Hopkins entered either a vase or a basket of carnations, and sometimes both. For four years running, 1926 to 1929, their carnations carried off first prize.

Their house in Hove Street was built by Mr A. Chadwell, who was also responsible for the erection of several others overlooking Kingsway. The Chadwells lived in the first house south of Hove Manor called Iver House. A member of the family, Miss Chadwell, perhaps even a cousin, married into the Bungard family – funeral directors.

Hove Street still retained its rural aspect in the early 1920s. Opposite no. 42 were some old farm buildings, and Joyce enjoyed helping an elderly man feed his pigeons there. On this site the electricity generating station, the fire station and the post office sorting office were later built. After the latter went up, young Joyce, whose bedroom was at the front of the house, was woken every morning by the sound of activity opposite as the men made an early start sorting letters. As for the fire station, the family rather enjoyed its proximity. Her father waited for days to catch the sight of the fire engine emerging through those giant doors for the first time, while Joyce liked to watch the drill, especially when it involved climbing the tower and there were hoses spouting water in splendid arcs. The fire station was previously sited in George Street, but it was rather a confined space in which to turn an engine and couple the horses before speeding off to a fire. Various pieces of fire-fighting equipment were kept dotted about the town; one depot used to be a small cottage next door to the Connaught pub.

FIRST

Brighton, Hove & Sussex Horticultural Society.

SUMMER SHOW, JULY 3rd & 4th, 1929.

EXHIBIT:	CLASS:
3 Vases Carnations	41

EXHIBITOR:

Mr. E. D. HOPKINS,

Wokingham Lodge, Hove Street,

Hove.

First Prize carnations.
(Hopkins)

Further south down Hove Street on the east side stood the venerable Hove Manor with its gardens and high flint walls. Many notable people stayed there including the Prince of Wales – in fact two holders of that office, the Prince Regent and the Duke of Windsor. Betty Stringer remembered looking down from the top floor of her house in Church Road and seeing the Prince of Wales and the Duke of York (later George VI) walking in the grounds. This would have been sometime between 1919 and 1921 when there were several royal visits. Hove Manor was later offered to Hove Corporation, which unfortunately declined because they were too anxious about the possible burden on the rates, and so it was demolished in the 1930s.

Then Hove Street was straightened, the old Ship Inn demolished and set further back, and the road was set with wooden blocks. While this was going on piece by piece, a night watchman kept an eye on things in his little shelter, and Mrs Hopkins would supply him with hot drinks. The street lighting was also improved, and it seems that Hove Council wanted to install a bracket lamp attached to no. 42. But Mr and Mrs Hopkins were not in favour, to say the least, and there were various ratepayers association protest meetings. In the event the bracket lamp never went up, and instead tall poles were erected on either side of the road to hold a pendant lamp in the middle.

Lastly, to complete the transition of Hove Street, the old Hove College (founded 1796) on the south-west corner with its adjacent old-fashioned sweet shop were demolished and a large block of flats called Viceroy Lodge built on the site. Hove College moved to Lansworth House, a red brick mansion, not far off in the Kingsway, which was previously occupied by a mentally ill man of good family and his carer. The row of coastguard cottages south-east of the Ship Inn were also demolished.

There was once a scheme to erect a Hove Pier and plans were far enough advanced for a pile-laying ship to arrive at Hove. But it was not long before a gale swept in and beached it. The event caused great excitement and Joyce and her cousin down from London spent hours on the beach just looking. She cannot remember whether the ship was floated off or just broke up, but she rather thinks it was the latter.

The west-facing frontage of Hove Manor. (Brighton & Hove Libraries)

William Lynn, his wife and daughter outside the Ship Inn, c. 1912. He was landlord from 1911 to 1920. (Shaw)

Hove College with the old name of the house, Cliff House, still visible. (Jeeves)

A memorable event took place on 20 July 1929. Mrs Hopkins, Joyce and her friend Hilda had taken a picnic tea to the beach and the children were happily digging in the sand with their small spades. There was a great expanse of sand because the tide was abnormally low and the weather was very hot and oppressive. Perhaps it was some sixth sense but Mrs Hopkins decided they must go home at once because there was a storm brewing – the children moaned of course as they did not want to leave, but many other families were also gathering up their belongings and moving off the beach. Meanwhile, a black ridge appeared on the horizon and soon the sea came rushing in powered by a tidal wave. It was a terrifying experience and there was no warning of what was to happen. Local boatmen said the wave was bad enough, but the backwash was even worse because the water appeared to be boiling. Joyce remembered seeing quantities of deck chairs and other debris from the beach floating on the sea, and she believed there were some casualties.

An annual event much looked forward to was the arrival of the circus, which pitched its big top on the site now covered by the King Alfred. Joyce used to try hard to stay awake until 10 p.m. to hear the big bang when a man was shot out of a cannon. One year there was a sensation when a barber, for the sake of a wager, undertook to shave a man in the lion's den.

For a short time Joyce attended a small private school called Corseley House at 53 Sackville Road; the school colours were green and cream. At that time there were many small private schools in Hove. One of her friends was Mary Blogg who in later years ran the Sackville School of Music. Then there were Patricia and Jose Colwell, members of an old Hove family, and Betty Stringer who later worked as a librarian at Hove Library for many years.

Coastguard Cottages on the Kingsway. (Jeeves)

Joyce on the canal in her very own rowing boat in the 1920s. (Hopkins)

The Stringers kept a shop in George Street where you could buy practically anything. Muriel Wright also attended Corseley House and her parents ran a furnishing firm in Blatchington Road that later became Vokins. Joyce completed her education at Brighton and Hove High School for Girls where she said she enjoyed every minute. Soon after she left Corseley House the school moved to St Aubyns, where it was known as St Katherine's, and the school colours were pink and brown.

In the 1930s Joyce was the proud possessor of her very own rowing boat – a gift from her father who was fond of yachting and was a member of the Sussex Yacht Club at Southwick. She learned to row in the calmer waters of the canal. The rowing boat was kept on the beach in front of wherever the family's beach hut was located – usually in the Welbeck Avenue area. It was never on its own resting on the beach, because there were usually some canoes for company. There were also plenty of young helpers eager to assist in launching the boat or hauling it up the beach. Joyce recalls, 'Hours beyond number were spent with others on the boat, in it, off it, swimming, etc.' Those halcyon days ended in September 1939.

Meanwhile, the Hopkins family was finding Hove Street too busy for their taste and moved to 1 Welbeck Avenue. Perhaps it was not the best time to move, because they were there during the Second World War and at times it felt like being in the front line. Joyce was married from that house in November 1945. Soon afterwards her parents moved to a rebuilt bomb-damaged house at 110 New Church Road.

30

Vera Messenger

Parlour Maid to General Gordon's Niece

John Messenger came to Hove in the 1880s – no doubt thinking it would be a good town in which to use his carpentry skills with the extensive house-building taking place. His first address was in Belfast Street, but he later moved to Shirley Street and eventually to Haddington Street. He and his wife Emma had four children, and their son Alfred was born in 1885 when they were living in Shirley Street. He was educated at the George Street Schools (later renamed St Andrew's School), and when he grew up earned his living not far from the school in an ironmonger's shop at 34 George Street, Hove, where he stayed for thirty-four years. He became the manager and E.J.J. Thompson was his boss. Mr Thompson was elected to Hove Council in 1910 and was Mayor of Hove from 1930 to 1932. In 1936 he was elected Alderman. Mr Thompson was associated with the start of the Rutland Hall Mission Church and was Superintendent of it for some twenty-five years.

Alfred Messenger married Elizabeth, who was a dressmaker, and the couple had three children – Alfred George (1911–88), John Stanley (1914–95) and Vera who was born in 1920. The second son may have been named Stanley after H.S. Messenger who was killed in the First World War and whose name appears on the brass memorial tablets in the vestibule of Hove Library. Like their father the children all attended the George Street Schools and then finished with a spell at the East Hove Schools.

Vera often used to pop in to see her father at the shop. One day Miss Gordon asked Mr Messenger if he knew of a girl who could help out with the spring-cleaning. He thought it would be a suitable task for Vera, so off she went. It seems Miss Gordon liked her, because she was asked to stay on permanently. She continued to live at home and walked to Miss Gordon's residence daily.

Miss Gordon's uncle was General Charles George Gordon (1833–85), who was a great hero of the Victorian Age. Indeed out of all the interesting people General Wolseley met throughout the course of a very active life, he singled out General Gordon and General Lee as the two men he most admired. (Many of Wolseley's papers are stored in Hove Library and his sisters lived at Medina Villas.) The centenary of Gordon's birth was celebrated at Hove in 1933 by a special exhibition at Hove Museum. Miss Gordon and the general's nephew, Colonel L.A. Gordon, lent several relics, including the tools he took with him to China.

Rutland Mission Hall, 1906. (Author)

Miss Gordon lived in some state at 27 Wilbury Road from about 1915 to 1937. When Vera arrived there as parlour maid, the household staff consisted of Kate, the resident housekeeper, and a cook. Vera had to pay for her own uniform, which consisted of a black dress worn with a frilly apron on top and of course a white cap. She helped to serve meals in the impressive dining room and was paid about 10s a week. It amused her somewhat when Miss Gordon had finished eating and pretended to have forty winks. In reality she was keeping a sharp look out to make sure everything was done according to custom – this included sweeping crumbs off properly with a little brush and folding the tablecloth exactly along the creases. Miss Gordon also had the habit of running her fingers along the banisters to make sure the stairs had been dusted. One of Vera's tasks was to read the newspaper to Miss Gordon who was unable to see the small print, and when the housekeeper had the day off Vera would make sure Miss Gordon got to bed safely. Another of Vera's duties was to answer the door, and she remembers admitting a Colonel – perhaps it was Colonel Wishart who lived nearby at Wilbury Lawn, 44 Wilbury Road. Another frequent visitor was Miss Gordon's sister, Lady Prinney, who was a kind, sweet soul. But she suffered from gallstones and often had to hold a hot water bottle to her side to relieve the symptoms. In spite of her strictness, Miss Gordon was a kind old lady, and when Vera left some four years later she received a very pretty little brooch with a mounted green stone as a parting gift. The cook was quite put out by the present, declaring it was far too good for a mere parlour maid.

Alfred Messenger died in 1956, and Vera says sadly that her grandparents now lie under the service road on the west side of George Street. But on the brighter side, she is impressed by the brand new St Andrew's School, which she was invited to tour when it was finished, along with other nearby residents.

31

Frank Mainstone

The Duke of Portland's Bailiff

Frank Mainstone's name sounds deceptively ordinary. In fact his Christian names were Francis Ignatius Dominic and the family's original surname was de Maintenon – it claimed descent from Françoise d'Aubigné, Marquise de Maintenon (1635–1719) who became the second wife of Louis XIV of France. When the French Revolution broke out, the family thought it would be prudent to move to England and they anglicised their name to Mainstone.

Frank Mainstone became bailiff for the lands at Aldrington and Hove owned by the 6th Duke of Portland (1857–1943). The Duke did not set out to be a landowner in the Portslade and Hove area; he acquired the land through default of mortgage. The land stretched from Old Shoreham Road to Kingsway and Mr Mainstone arranged the sale of some land to Hove Council. It is interesting to find that Frank had some other enterprises on the side. For instance, in July 1896 it was noted by Hove Council that he had set up a wooden hut on wheels with a corrugated roof, west of St Philip's Church, without obtaining planning permission. It was used to sell refreshments, but the council insisted it be pulled down. Frank also used to keep a pig in a pit where Stoneham Park Recreation Ground is today. He and another man owned the pig jointly until one day when both man and pig vanished. Later on Mr Mainstone built up a large pig farm where Wish Road is today, and he also owned some fields, which he let to the travelling circus every year. In January 1914 Frank Mainstone presented Hove Council with 1,000 wallflower plants to put in their recreation grounds.

Frank and his family lived in a cottage in a lane that later became Mainstone Road. When they lived there fields surrounded the cottage. Apparently the Duke of Portland asked Hove Council if they would honour his bailiff when the road was made up, and they did. The Mainstones had a family of twelve children including Winnie, Edith, Frank, Fred, Percy, Bert, Cyril, Mabel and Willy. Mabel died at the age of six in 1899 during an outbreak of diphtheria and Willy died of tuberculosis aged four. All the children attended Aldrington School. Mrs Mainstone watched from her bedroom window as the foundation stone of Holy Cross Church was laid – in those days it was the Parish Hall of St Philip's Church, and it opened in 1903. Mrs Mainstone had just given birth to George, her twelfth child. Wally later lived in

Burgess Hill, Frank became a pig farmer in Portslade, Percy was a greengrocer in Blatchington Road, Bert went to Australia to work on the Sydney Bridge and stayed on while the youngest child, Cyril, became a carpenter. Frank managed to set all his children up in life by giving them a parcel of land each on which to build a house. Cyril and his wife Irene with his unmarried sister Winnie lived in a bungalow built on one such plot of land in North Road, Portslade, that had formerly been a field where quoits were played. It must have been a squash, as there were three children there as well. But during the Second World War Winnie worked for the NAAFI and so was away a great deal of the time.

Index

Abinger Road 19, 20, 25, 27, 76, 79, 119
Adders' Bottom 112
Adur Terrace, Southwick 102
Albion Street 104
Albourne 10
Aldrington Recreation Ground 50, *see also* Wish Meadow
Aldrington School 156
Allen, Pte 81
Applesham Way 55
Ashurst 11
Atherfold, Mrs 79
Ayres, Charlie 72

Bampfield Street 24, 39
Banfield, Jack 8
Batholomews 20
Beach Bungalows 85
Beach House 94
Belfast pub 47, 154
Belfast Street 47
Bellman's 114
Benfield Valley 16
Benfield Way 18, 107
Blaber, Daisy 67
Blaker, Edward 15
Blatchington Road 47, 140, 143, 153, 157
Blogg, Mary 152
Boundary Road, Hove 49, 51, 98, 99, 123
Brambledean Road 103
Brasslands Drive 13
Brighton 20, 48, 102, 133, 146
Brighton & Hove Bus Co. 106
Brighton & Hove Operatic Society 132
Britannia Flour Mills 93, 96, 111
Broadbank, Reg 58, 59
Brooker Hall 94
Brooker, Mr 105
Broomfield, John 7, 11, 12, 13, 14, 41, 99

Brown, Dr 72
Bungard, Mr 74, 148
Bunting, Miss 103
Burgess Hill 10, 157
Burn, J.W. 58, 59, 80
Butt, Dame Clara 140
Butt, John Eede 98

Cabbage Field 107
Caffyn, Capt 48
Cambridge Grove 40
Cameron, Jock 81
Cameronians 119
Canadian soldiers 14, 30, 31, 70, 84, 90, 113
Chadwell, A. 149
Chalky Road 72
Champion House 111
Chappell, Sidney 76, 77
Church Road, Hove 125, 126, 146
Church Road, Portslade 96, 103, 104, 105, 111, 113
Clarendon pub 63
Clarendon Place, Portslade 62, 63
Clarendon Villas 144
Cleverley, June 107, 108
Cockroost Hill 14, 16, 98
Collona 134
Colonel (horse) 47
Connaught pub 149
Connaught Road Schools 52, 105, 112, 142
Co-op 58, 59, 60, 80, 141, 143
Copperas Gap 98
Corfield, Mr 94
Corseley House 152, 153
Cowper Street 73
Cox & Barnard 144
Crab House 98, 111
Crown pub 97, 98
Cutty Sark 133
CVA (engineering firm) 74, 109

Dabs 111
Dean, Dixie 81
Dearing, Amy 16
Denmark Road 28
Devil's Dyke 10, 16, 107, 112, 113, 142
Downland Court 71
Drew, Charlie 62
Dudeney, Peggy 56
Dudeney's Laundry 25
Dugay, Pam 107
Dunker, Dr 64
Dyer, Mr 146
Dyke Hovel 10, 83

Earl, Miss 64
East Hove Boys' School 64, 144
East Hove Senior Boys' School 105
East Street, Portslade 91
Easthill 11, 15, 19
Easthill Park 77
Eaton Road 64
Ellen Street School, Hove 142
Ellen Street, Portslade 117
Elm Road 25, 28
Emery, printer 62, 146–7
Eutopia 116, 117

Fairway Crescent 107, 109
F.E. Webb 93
Felton, Mr 32
Ferry 94, 111
Field, Mr 92
First Avenue 133
First World War 19, 21, 22, 25, 49, 62, 67, 92, 94, 101, 125, 154
Flynn's 110, 111
Four Winds 136
Fowler, T.H. 32, 36
Franklin Road 46, 47, 48, 85
Fulking 9, 12
Fulking Furze 10

Garrard, Leslie 46
Gates, Arthur 49
General Strike 35, 103
George pub 13, 14
George Street, Hove 73, 124–32,
 141, 142, 145, 149, 153, 154
German PoWs 12, 50, 94, 95
Gigin's Bakery 46
Gilbert & Sullivan Society 132
Gladstone Road 121
Goatcher's Buttercup Field 107
Goble, Mr 113
Godfray, Fred 46
Godwin, Miss 18
Golden Grove 133
Goldstone Villas 144
Green, R. (developers) 31
Grigson, Len 25
Gut, the 111

Haddington Street 142, 154
Hallyburton Road 76
Hamblin, Charlie 111
Hangleton 142
Hannington's Depository 64
Harold Brown 56
Harrison, Ernie 37
Hart family 45
Haywards Heath 16
Helena Close 29
Hell Fire Corner 71
Hemsworth, Revd N.E.C. 29
Henfield 10
Hess, Myra 140
High Street 13, 67, 68, 70, 71
Hilton, Wag 8
Hindenburg (Zeppelin) 143
HMS Britannia 116
HMS Edinburgh 116
HMS Excellent 118
HMS Hood 106
HMS King Alfred 114, 115
HMS Pioneer 113
HMS Vernon 38
HMS Vincent 118
Holder, Nurse 102, 105
Holy Cross Church 156
Home Guard 81–4, 113
Hore Belisha's Militia 59
Horsted Keynes 109
Hove 93
Hove College 150, 151

Hove County School for Boys 143, 144
Hove Fire Station 126, 150
Hove Grammar School for Girls 109
Hove Library 147, 153, 154
Hove Lions Day 123
Hove Manor 150, 151
Hove Museum 154
Hove Pier 150
Hove Street 133, 136, 149–53
Hove Training Home for Girls 143,
 144
Huggett, Mr 71
Huggett, Mrs 13
Hutson, Mrs 143, 144

J.B. Paddon 93
Jenner, Mrs 67
Jigs, Moulds & Tool Co. 113
John Miles 50, 93
John Player & Co. 116, 117
Jolly (horse) 7, 8
Jolly Sailors pub 106
Joseph, Sister 100
Joymanco 40
Jupp, Mr 71

Kaye, Miss 103
Kearny & Trecker 74
Kells, W.R. 28
Kingsway 149, 150, 156

Lady Bee Yard 80, 136
Lansdowne Place 77
LB&SC Railway 106
Leader 136, 137
Leicester Villas 70
Lewonski, Mr 126, 145
Licence, Ellen 45
Lindup, Mr 71
Livingstone Road Baths 142
Lloyd, George 10
Lloyd, Mr 142
Locks Hill 21
Ludwig Reediman 95
Lyon & Hall 140, 144

Mackarness, Joe 9
Maggie 133
Mainstone Road 156
Manetta, Madame 73
Manor Hall Road 20
Mappin & Webb 108

Mason, Mr 71
Maypole's 141
Medina Place 139
Medina Villas 154
Melrose Avenue 79
Metal Box Factory 32
Mile Oak 9, 11, 67, 111, 113
Mile Oak Farm 15
Mile Oak Gardens 100
Mile Oak Road 71, 72, 100
Mile Oak Waterworks 17, 19, 66, 83,
 98, 112
Miles, Frederick 62, 97
Miles, John 89, 97
Miles, W. & Co. 127, 128
Mill Cottages 19
Mill Lane 29, 109
Mitchell, Marie 101
Montgomery Street 140, 142
Montpelier Road, Brighton 115
Mulberry Harbour 84
Mystery Towers 102

Nab Lighthouse 102
Nell, Captain 100
New Barn Farm 8
New Church Road 47, 48, 104, 153
Newick 7, 10
Norden, Mr 143
North Lane 60
North Road 119, 157
North Street 62, 63, 96, 104, 105,
 113
Norway Street 48, 74

Oden, Dorothy 27
Old Shoreham Road, Hove 100, 156
Old Shoreham Road, Portslade 19,
 35, 55, 67, 113
Orme, Bob 112, 113
Osborne Villas 136

Pashley, Cecil 97, 98
Pavilion cinema 105
Payne, Walter 130
Peacehaven 109
Peacey, Mrs 144
Penfold, Mr 92
Petersfield Laundry 67, 68
Pettyfer, Roy 130
Phoebe Hessell 136
Picturedrome cinema 105

Portland Road 40, 58, 67, 145
Portslade Fire Station 25
Portslade Gas Works 25, 86–9, 91–5, 118
Portslade Grange 15
Portslade Industrial School 28, 71, 72, 83
Portslade Post Office 112
Portslade Rotary Club 18, 56
Portslade Station 83
Portsmouth 38, 45, 84, 102, 103, 149
Poynings 10
President Briand 56
Princess 136, 138
Purdy, Miss 37

Ralph, Mr 112
Rawson, Sir Cooper 137
Read, Hector 24
Reed family 22, 23
Ronuk 32–7, 75, 77
Rook, Mr 71
Rosebud 93
Rudgwick 11
Rutland Mission Hall 154, 155
Rutter, Mr 94
Rye 38

Sackville Gardens 115
St Andrew's Church, Portslade 28, 50, 97
St Andrew's Road 62, 64, 65, 102
St Andrew's School, Hove 154, 155
St Andrew's School, Portslade 24, 51, 58, 64, 89, 91, 97, 103, 110
St Andrew's Youth Club 85, 86
St Aubyns 153
St Aubyn's Road 110
St Barnabas's Church 59, 60
St John Ambulance Brigade 88
St Katherine's 153
St Leonard's Church 50, 62, 85
St Nicolas's Church 18, 23, 24, 29, 41, 98
St Nicholas's Road 101
St Nicolas's School 20, 28, 49, 50, 58, 59, 75, 79, 107
St Peter's Infants' School
St Philip's Church 50, 97, 156
St Winifred's School 64
Sayers, Mrs 75
Scutt, Reg 37

Sea-spray 133
Second World War 16, 30, 31, 43, 48, 55, 59, 64, 81–4, 90, 95, 106, 109, 112–15, 119, 130, 144, 153, 157
Sharpethorne Crescent 107
Shell Brit 56
Shell Wharf 56
Shelldale Crescent 119
Shelldale Road 25
Shemeld, Margaret 130
Shepherd & Dog pub 9, 112
Ship Inn 150, 151
Shirley Street 154
Shoreham 56, 81, 83, 97, 112
Silverthorne, Gracie 62
Slonk Hill 83
Smallbone, Mr 94
Smith, Moffat 9
Smith, Sundius 96
Smokey House 15
Smugglers 98, 111
Southdown Avenue 60
Southdown Bus Co. 101, 103
Southdown Foxhounds 9, 10
Southdown Road 15
Southern Cross 24
Southern Cross pub 25
Southern Cross Mission 39
Southern Railway 107
Southwick 98, 117, 153
Southwick Home Guard 83, 84
Stag's Head pub 14, 28
Stallabrass, Dennis 40
Stallabrass, Marianne 41
Stanley Avenue 60
Star Model Laundry 62, 97
Station Road 46, 81, 83, 96, 99, 123
Steyning 93
Stockwell Orphanage 101
Stoneham Park 156
Stonery 15, 18, 22
Stonery Road 71
Stringer, Betty 150
Sussex Road 136
Sussex Yacht Club 18, 153
Sweetheart 133

Tanner, Albert 55
Tarbrett, Mr 143
Tauber, Richard 140
Territorial Army 49, 59, 113
Tester, Jack 8

Thompson, E.J.J. 154
Thorpe, Mr 143
Tidy, Daisy 69, 70
Tidy, John 67, 69
Tilling, Thomas 58, 103
Toye, Daniel 127
Toye, Gladys 127
Trafalgar Road 39, 119
Trigwell, Mr 11, 92
Truleigh Hill 19
Tubb, H.W. 39, 63, 69, 102, 117, 120
Turner, M.G. 17

Uckfield 70
Unity Youth Club 88
Upper Market Street 131
Upperton, William 126
Uridge, Dick 7

Vale Park 75, 104, 111, 119
Vale Road 104
Valley Road 11, 71
Ventnor Villas 127
Victoria Recreation Ground 55
Victoria Road 74, 76
Victoria Terrace 45
Virgo, Mary Ann 91
Vokins 153
Volks Railway 106

War Memorial, Portslade 121
Ward, William 78
Watson, Miss 75
Welbeck Avenue 153
Weller family 119
Wellington Road 76, 85, 88, 98, 106, 111
West, Sid 7, 17
Western Road, Brighton 65
Wilbury Road 155
Willard, Jess 63
Windlesham Close 57
Windley, Bill 10
Windmill pub 84
Wish Meadow (Wish Park) 127
Wish Road 156
Wishart, Colonel 155
Wolseley, General 154
Wolseley Road 39, 73, 79
Worthing 40, 56
Worthing Gas Co. 94